The UN Convention on the Rights of the Child

The UK's First Report to the UN Committee on the Rights of the Child

February 1994

Contents

Introduction

i   There is an increasing understanding in the UK of the importance of providing children with a good start in life and ensuring that their material and emotional needs are met. It is our aim that every child should be able to enjoy a secure and happy childhood. Such a childhood has a value of its own but it also provides the best preparation for adult life and for empowering children to participate fully in society.

ii   The UK's perception of children's rights and needs is closely aligned to the philosophy of the Convention. The UK accepts that, because they are vulnerable, children are entitled to special consideration and protection. As they become older and more mature they must increasingly be allowed to make decisions about matters concerning them.

iii   The UK, while not complacent, can claim with some confidence to have a good record in general on its treatment of children. It is also a record on which we are constantly seeking to build with the steady introduction of measures to improve children's lives in a wide range of areas.

iv   The National Health Service provides high quality health care for adults and children alike, regardless of income, generally free at the point of delivery. Pregnancy and childbirth have never been safer. There has been a steady reduction in infant mortality rates. There has been sustained improvement in children's health with an increasing emphasis on a strategy based on prevention. Our successful immunisation programme has been responsible for a very considerable reduction in childhood infectious disease.

v   Free primary and secondary education is every child's right together with higher education for those suitably qualified and motivated to benefit from it. 55% of our 17 year-olds are in some form of further education and about 30% of the relevant age group are in higher education. Recent legislative changes have sought to raise the standards of education for all children. They have increased opportunities for parents to provide appropriate direction and guidance in respect of their children's education through increased choice and more say in the running of schools. Additional measures have been introduced to secure improvements for children with special educational needs.

vi   The structure of our Social Security benefits enables the Government to focus help effectively on those groups, such as families, who face the greatest pressure. Those on very low earnings are eligible for benefits which boost their income. Child benefit, a universal benefit, which is usually paid direct to the mother, makes an effective contribution to the family budget. It is recognised that families who have a child with disabilities incur additional expenses. There are several special allowances payable to help families to meet these extra demands on their budget. A new allowance is to be introduced to help parents receiving family credit to pay for child care costs.

vii   So far as the law on the care and upbringing of children in England and Wales is concerned we have in the Children Act 1989 legislation which clearly reflects the principles of the Convention. It brings together in one statute both the public and the private law. It makes clear that, except on adoption, parents never lose responsibility for their children. It seeks to ensure that the welfare of the child is the paramount consideration when arrangements are being made for the care of children following divorce or separation of the parents and that the child's wishes are taken into account. This is an important safeguard for an increasing number of children where the divorce rate has been rising in the UK.

viii   The Act recognises that whenever possible children are best brought up by their parents in their own home. It places a duty on local authorities to provide services for children in need to help parents bring up their children. When it is necessary for courts and local authorities to intervene in children's lives they are required to have the child's welfare as their first consideration. A local authority looking after a child has a duty to plan effectively for the child and to keep the plan under review to ensure the child's best interests are served. The Act provides for the regulation of foster placements and for the registration and inspection of children's homes and day care provision so that when children are away from their parents their welfare can be safeguarded.

ix   In Northern Ireland child care law is being revised to bring it broadly into line with the position in England and Wales under the Children Act 1989. In Scotland the welfare of the child is at the centre of the child care provisions of the Social Work (Scotland) Act 1968. In a recent White Paper "Scotland's Children" the Government have proposed a number of changes in the law and in policy, which reflect the principles of the UN Convention.

x   The Government is conscious of the need always to be vigilant to identify areas where there are deficiencies in our arrangements for children and to take steps to tackle them. In the UK we have a large number of voluntary organisations which campaign vigorously to improve the lot of children. Some of the organisations were the original providers of children's services which are now statutory. There is a history of partnership between these bodies and Government - a partnership not without its tensions. Nonetheless Government acknowledges the value of their contribution.

xi   The Government recognises the particular needs of children and will continue through legislation, policy and practice to strive to promote the best interests of children in accordance with the Articles of the Convention.

xii   The United Kingdom's overseas development assistance policy is closely related to the Convention on the Rights of the Child. In addition to bilateral aid programmes, the Government is a major contributor to multilateral development agencies whose work benefits children. These include the United Nations Fund for Children (UNICEF), the World Health Organisation (WHO), the United Nations Population Fund (UNPFA) and the World Food Programme (WFP). The Overseas Development Administration also cooperates closely with the World Bank, Regional Development Banks and the European Community. In each of these agencies the United Kingdom is active in promoting a greater focus upon helping the poorest and most vulnerable sections of society.

Chapter 1: General Measures of Implementation

1.1   The United Kingdom signed the Convention on 19 April 1990 and ratified it on 16 December 1991. It entered into force for the UK on 15 January 1992. On ratification the United Kingdom entered a number of reservations and declarations. These are set out at Annex A to the Report.

Harmonising National law and Policy with the provisions of the Convention

1.2   The United Kingdom is a unitary state and comprises England and Wales, Scotland and Northern Ireland. Scotland and to some extent Northern Ireland have separate legal systems from that applying in England and Wales, but similar principles apply throughout the United Kingdom. We have indicated in the report where a provision refers to England and Wales, or Scotland, or Northern Ireland. If no indication has been given, it can be assumed that the provision applies to the UK as a whole.

1.3   Ratification of the Convention did not require any amendment to UK legislation. It is accepted, however, that there is a continuing need to take active measures to ensure that the aims of legislation are translated into everyday policy and practice throughout the country. Ratification of the Convention will help to ensure that the needs and interests of children are given a high profile across government.

1.4   The Department of Health was given responsibility for coordinating the United Kingdom's response to the United Nations Committee on the Rights of the Child on implementation of the Convention. Following ratification the Department wrote to all government departments reminding them that they had an obligation to ensure that legislation and policy for which they were responsible reflected the principles set out in the Convention. They were asked to review their position and consider what changes if any they needed to make to comply.

1.5   In major areas affecting children, departments have taken measures since implementation of the Convention which bring policy more into line with the Convention. Some of the more significant developments are discussed in this chapter.

The Children Act

1.6   One particularly important initiative was the establishment, shortly after the Act came into force, of a strategy for monitoring the implementation of the Children Act 1989, the current legislation governing the care and upbringing of children in England and Wales. It accords very closely with the principles in the Convention. In particular it shares with the Convention two overarching principles namely that the best interests of the child should be the first consideration and the voice of the child should be heard.

1.7   The Children Act Advisory Committee was set up to monitor the workings of the court related aspects of the Act. The Committee reports each year on their findings to the Lord Chancellor, the Home Secretary, the Secretaries of State for Health and for Wales and the President of the Family Division of the High Court.   The Secretaries of State for Health and for Wales are also required to report to Parliament on the implementation of the Act. This report is informed by statistical collections, research findings and inspections and studies undertaken by the Social Services Inspectorate in England and Wales, professional divisions of the Department of Health and Welsh Office. Both Reports are published and distributed widely. It follows that the operation of the Children Act and its effect on children is subject to regular and public scrutiny.

1.8   The findings at the end of the first year of the Act being in operation were for the most part favourable. The principles of the Act were in general being reflected in practice. There was evidence that local authorities were providing a range of services to families experiencing difficulties thereby helping them to bring up their children themselves. Children were thus increasingly able to remain safely within their own family.   Fewer children were being subjected to the trauma of being removed from their homes. The welfare of children was being safeguarded and promoted more effectively than before.

1.9   In some areas , however, there was room for improvement if children's best interests are to be served. It was evident that some authorities had been slow to develop adequate initiatives for children in need. Other authorities needed to improve their arrangements for preparing children for leaving care and their after-care services.

1.10   It is too early to reach a considered judgement about the second year of the Act's operation but early indications suggest that the progress made in many areas has been built on.

Child Care law in Scotland

1.11   The main changes which are proposed in law and policy are outlined in the recent White Paper "Scotland's Children", which not only responded to the recommendations of a number of specific reports and the views on them expressed during consultation, but took account of the principles of the UN Convention. The White Paper will be implemented by changes in primary legislation, by regulations and by guidance. New legislation will be introduced when there is sufficient Parliamentary time.

Child Care law in Northern Ireland

1.12   A proposal for a draft Children (Northern Ireland) Order was issued by the Department of Health and Social Services and the Office of Law Reform in July 1993, with a closing date of 30 November 1993 for comment. The draft Order is designed to reform and consolidate most of the public and private law relating to the care, upbringing and protection of children and the provision of personal social services for children in need (including disabled children) and their families.

1.13   Subject to Parliamentary approval at Westminster, the proposed Children (Northern Ireland) Order, will replace care provisions in the Children and Young Persons Act (Northern Ireland) 1968 as the main legislative basis for the provision of child care services in Northern Ireland. It will also reform the law relating to illegitimacy along the lines of the Family Law Reform Act 1987 in England and Wales.   The Order will be broadly similar to the Children Act 1989 and as such many of its underlying principles will be consistent with those of the Convention.

Residential Care for Children

1.14   In England the field of residential child care was one which had given increasing cause for concern   during the late eighties and into the early nineties. There had been a succession of well publicised scandals in children's homes where children's rights to proper care had been violated. The Government responded by setting up two independent inquiries. The first was chaired by Sir William Utting, the former Chief Inspector of the Social Services Inspectorate and the second by Norman Warner, former Director of Social Services, Kent County Council. They reported in July 1991 and December 1992 respectively. The findings of both enquiries, although focused on slightly different areas, were sharply critical of the service which was being provided for children.

1.15   The Government accepted that there was an urgent need to improve the quality of care.   A timetabled programme was drawn up for implementing the recommendations of both inquiries so as to tackle the range of deficiencies identified. The aspects requiring the most immediate attention were the recruitment, selection and appointment of staff and the arrangements for staff supervision and appraisal. Local authorities were instructed to improve their procedures in these areas without delay and to report back to Ministers on their progress. The indications are that substantial improvements have now been achieved, but the position will continue to be kept under review

1.16   One of the most significant developments coming out of the Warner

Inquiry was the establishment by the Government in September 1993 of a Children's Residential Care Support Force. Led by a former Director of Social Services, it has a core membership of professionals and lay people from a wide range of disciplines, including education. Its role is to advise and assist local authorities in England and Wales to help to bring about necessary changes in management and personnel practices. The Support Force will report back to Ministers on its operation in the spring of 1994.

1.17 In Wales, local authorities were additionally required to develop a strategy for residential care in accordance with the recommendations of the Welsh Office report "Accommodating Children".

1.18 One important recommendation of the Utting Report had implications that went beyond residential care. This was that local authorities should be asked to prepare and publish plans for children's services. These plans would help to improve services for children by creating the foundation for the planning, management and review of child care services. They would encourage authorities to make their policies more explicit and to ensure that resource allocations reflected policies. They would make clear the extent to which the voluntary and private sector's services would be required to achieve a full range of provision. They would encourage collaboration between the voluntary and private sector and the authorities. They would assist the voluntary and private sector by allowing them to tailor the services to meet unfilled needs. They would assist with more effective monitoring of the service provision and help to ensure that could be readily adapted to cope with changing needs.

1.19 The Department of Health issued formal advice in November 1992 that local authorities in England which had not yet introduced plans should take steps to do so. Progress on the action taken in this area by authorities is being reviewed by the Department of Health's Social Services Inspectorate. A report will be published in Spring 1994.

1.20 In Scotland a major review of residential care culminated in the report "Another Kind of Home" which made a number of recommendations for improvement which cover professional qualifications and training, accommodation and regimes. In accepting the main recommendations, the Government have emphasised the need for close communication with young people in residential care and the need to respond to the views of young people in designing programmes of care.

Day Care Services

1.21 In England there are many types of day care services, which gives parents some choice. In recent years the numbers of day nurseries and child minders have increased quite significantly. By 1992 there were 91,600 places in day nurseries, and 108,000 registered child minders with over 250,000 places. There were 17,000 sessional day care services -

playgroups used by children aged 3 or 4 - with 409,000 places. 9 out of 10 children will have gone to some form of group activity - nursery education, playgroup or day nursery - before they reach 5, compulsory school age.

1.22 In Scotland the Government encourages a similar variety of provision for under 5s by local authorities, voluntary organisations and private organisations.

1.23 The various types of day care services in Wales have increased so that by 1992 there were 4,793 places in day nurseries, 3,851 registered child minders with over 10,000 places and 1,146 sessional day care services (playgroups) with 24,396 places used by children aged 3 or 4.

1.24 There has been a continuing improvement in the overall level of day care provision in Northern Ireland in the last few years. The number of places available at 31 March 1992 totalled 30,693 compared with 20,206 five years earlier. This is approximately equal to the UK average level of provision per 1,000 under 5s.

Adoption Law

1.25 In England and Wales, the biggest changes in adoption law for two decades were foreshadowed in the White Paper on Adoption published in November 1993. The paper sets out a modern framework for adoption to take account of the way people live now. It brings greater safeguards for adopted children. The principles underlying it are in harmony with those of the Convention. In particular it makes explicit that the first duty in adoption is to the child. Adoption is a service for children not adults. The White Paper proposes that children aged 12 or more should have the right to participate in their own adoption proceedings and to accept or reject an adoption. A Bill to give effect to the White Paper proposals will be introduced as soon as Parliamentary time permits.

1.26 Separate legislation is provided on adoption in Scotland. Following a recent review, the Government intends to publish proposals for improvements in the law and services for adoption and long-term care.

Children in conflict with the law

1.27 In the courts in England and Wales, two new measures have been introduced which are in close accord with the Convention. The Criminal Justice Act 1991 implemented in October 1992, brought certain significant benefits for young people. The upper age limit of the juvenile court was raised for sentencing purposes from 17 to 18, and the court was renamed the youth court. The Act also removed the sentence of detention in a Young Offender Institution for 14 year old boys, and set in place legislative measures designed to enable the ending of penal remands for 15 and 16

8

year old boys. This last measure can be implemented only when there is sufficient secure accommodation available; the Government has embarked on a programme to create the necessary places including a proposed new secure unit in Wales.

1.28 In Scotland most children who offend are referred to children's hearings and if grounds of referral are admitted or proved in court, the hearings decide what compulsory measures of care are needed in the child's best interests. Among the disposals available to children's hearings is secure accommodation, when a child is a danger to himself or to others or is likely to abscond. After age 16 young offenders are dealt with in the sheriff courts.

Child Witnesses

1.29 The Government took important steps to ease the burden of criminal proceedings for children who are the victims of or witnesses in cases of violence and sexual abuse in the Criminal Justice Act 1991. The Act implemented recommendations from the Committee on Video-Recorded Evidence, chaired by His Honour Judge Thomas Pigot. The main change is the use of pre-recorded video evidence in cases of violence and sexual abuse involving child witnesses.

1.30 Admitting video-recorded interviews in evidence reduces the need for the child to recount his or her evidence direct to the court. In order to preserve the rights of the accused, the child's account may need to be tested by cross-examination but the reforms allow that to take place from outside the courtroom by means of a live television link. The Act also prevents the accused from cross-examining the child in person and allows the Crown to by-pass magistrates' courts committal proceedings to speed up the process and reduce delays. It also sweeps away the legal presumption that children are not competent witnesses unless proved otherwise. Now evidence from a child witness is treated in the same way as evidence from an adult witness.

1.31 In order to help children who are to be witnesses in court, and their parents and carers, a child witness pack, based on research and examples of good practice from the UK and overseas has been prepared. It was funded by the Home Office, the Department of Health and the National Society for the Prevention of Cruelty to Children (NSPCC), Childline and the Calouste Gulbenkian Foundation - voluntary organisations concerned to promote the welfare of children.

1.32 The reforms described above are helping to ease the burden of criminal proceedings for child witnesses and to bring to justice those who commit crimes against children. The effect of the reforms is being closely monitored and if they are seen to fail abused children, the Government will look again at the options for further reform.

Disabled Children

1.33 The Government has a good record in providing help for families with disabled children - it is estimated that:

    i   the extension of help with care needs for children under 2 will help some 3,000 people at a cost of £6m (introduced in April 1990);

    ii   the new rates of Disability Living Allowance, for the less severely disabled, have already helped some 272,000 people including children;

    iii   increases in the child's disability premium will help about 20,000 at a cost of £8m (introduced in April 1990);

    iv   the introduction of the carer premium in April 1990, which includes help for caring for disabled children will help some 30,000 at a cost of £15m.

Special Educational Needs

1.34 In England and Wales, where the education of pupils with special educational needs is concerned, the Education Act 1981 already established the essential principles enshrined in paragraphs 2 and 3 of Article 23 of the Convention. The Government believes that the measures in the Education Act 1993 will further improve the education of children with special needs by:

    i   continuing to promote the integration of children with special needs into mainstream schools;

    ii   giving increased parental rights to express a preference for particular schools;

    iii   prescribing time limits for the assessment of such children; and

    iv   streamlining the procedures for appeal against perceived inadequate provision from LEAs.

1.35 The Government has also promoted, and will continue to promote, improved access for disabled children in mainstream schools.

Broadcasting

1.36 In the area of broadcasting, the Broadcasting Standards Council, a body established to consider the public's views on television programmes and to consider complaints relating to matters of taste and decency, has conducted research into the views of sixth form schoolchildren and will consider complaints from children and will allow children themselves to be represented in this administrative procedure.

Health

1.37 The Government's health promotion strategy "The Health of the Nation" launched in July 1992 selected 5 target areas : heart disease, cancers, mental illness, sexual health and accidents. The promotion of a healthy lifestyle in childhood is critical to the achievement of all the targets. The strategy recognises the need for a safe and healthy home environment in which children may develop to their full potential and commits the Government to the objective of ensuring that decent housing is within the reach of all families. There are a number of schemes, some directly funded by the Department of Health, designed to improve access to health services by homeless people, including families in bed and breakfast accommodation. All health regions are being asked this year to examine the adequacy of primary health care for homeless people which should help to accelerate progress.

1.38 In Wales the strategic approach differs. Strategic Intent and Direction for the NHS in Wales, initiated in 1989, seeks to achieve a level of health for people in Wales to compare with the best in Europe.

1.39 The infant mortality rate has been halved between 1978 and 1992. The Sudden Infant Death Syndrome rate has been halved between 1991 and 1992.

Co-ordinating children's policies and monitoring implementation of the Convention

1.40 Responsibility for policy on matters concerning children does not rest exclusively with one Government department. To improve coordination between departments several inter-departmental groups have been set up which meet regularly to take forward matters of mutual concern. These include the Inter-Departmental Group on Child Abuse, the Inter-Departmental Consultative Group on Provisions for under 5s, and the Home Office Steering Group on disclosure of convictions. Other ad-hoc groups meet as well. The Joint Action for Implementation Group which comprises representatives from the Department of Health, the local authorities and the voluntary child care sector meet regularly to review progress on implementation of the Children Act.

1.41 When consideration is being given to introducing new legislation or amending existing legislation or establishing new policy initiatives concerning children regular consultation takes place between the originating department and all other departments with an interest. This is done to try to ensure that all the implications and consequences of the changes are fully considered both at an early stage and continuously throughout the whole process.

1.42 The provision of statutory services for children in England and Wales is the responsibility of local authorities.

1.43 At local level too there is some evidence of increasing awareness of the need for and value of coordinating policies. The Children Act calls for the social services department to work together with the local education authority to review the provision of day care and child minding in their area. Social Services are to work together with education authorities and health authorities to ensure that appropriate services are provided to children in need. Local authorities are to work in partnership with the voluntary and private sector to provide a range of services in the area.

1.44 There is particular emphasis on joint working in the field of child protection. The Department of Health issued formal guidance known as "Working Together" to local authorities stressing the importance in this area of adopting working practices which are firmly based on inter-agency co-operation. Area Child Protection Committees are set up in every local authority area to ensure that the need is recognised for close working relationships between the Social Services Department, the police, Medical Practitioners, Community Health Workers, the Education Service and others who share a common aim to protect children at risk. The cooperation at individual case level is therefore supported by joint agency and management policies for child protection which are consistent with the policies and plans for the related service provision. The Area Child Protection Committee provides a forum for developing common monitoring and reviewing child protection policies.

1.45 The Department of Health, Home Office, Department for Education and Welsh Office are jointly producing guidance on inter-agency co-operation at local level in relation to the prevention and control of youth offending. This will be published early in 1994.

1.46 Every government department was asked to measure legislation and policy and practice in the field for which they have responsibility against the general principles of the Convention and against individual principles which were particularly relevant to them. This report is informed by their responses.

Publicising the provisions of the Convention under Article 42

1.47 Following ratification of the Convention the Department of Health and the Welsh Office sent a copy of the Convention to every local authority, Regional and District health authorities including NHS Trusts and to the major voluntary child care organisations in England and Wales. The organisations were advised that their policies and practice had to comply with the provisions of the Convention. There was a similar distribution of copies of the Convention in Northern Ireland. In Scotland departments brought the provisions of the Convention to the attention of their relevant agencies.

1.48 A booklet for the general public on the Convention "The Rights of the Child - A Guide to the UN Convention" was launched in February 1993. It was produced by the Department of Health in conjunction with the Children's Rights Development Unit, a voluntary organisation set up to monitor the UK's compliance with the Convention. In England and Wales the booklet was distributed to Citizen's Advice Bureaux, Libraries, Social Services Departments, small advice centres and Regional and District health authorities, including NHS Trusts. Similar distributions took place in Northern Ireland and Scotland. The booklet is attractively presented and sets out the Convention's Articles for children and adults in an easy-to-understand way.

1.49 The Department for Education has drawn the attention of schools specifically to the booklet.

Publicising this report under Article 44.6

1.50 The UK's report will be sent to every local authority and health authority including NHS Trusts. It will be circulated to all government departments. Voluntary child care organisations will receive a copy and copies will be placed in public libraries.

Chapter 2: Definition of the Child

Article 1

2.1   Under UK laws and regulations, the following ages of majority or legal minimum ages for the following circumstances apply:

Age of attainment of majority

2.2   18

Legal counselling without parental consent

2.3   A child of any age has the right to apply for the court's permission to start proceedings for residence or contact when they have sufficient understanding, under the Children Act 1989. A child of any age may sue in the court but it has to be done through a "next friend". At the age of 16 a child may apply for criminal legal aid in their own right or through their parents on their behalf. A child under 18 who wishes to apply for legal aid in civil proceedings must do so through an adult on their behalf but children are now assessed on their own means not that of their parents. A child may instruct his own solicitor under the Children Act provided that he has sufficient age and understanding.

Medical counselling without parental consent

2.4   Under the Children Act 1989 a child can refuse to consent to a psychiatric or medical examination or other assessment in proceedings for an interim care order, an emergency protection order or a child assessment order when he is of sufficient understanding. Following the Gillick case (*Gillick v West Norfolk and Wisbech Area Health Authority and another [1985] 3 AER 402*), children of any age have the right to give consent to clinical care and treatment providing they have the maturity to understand the implications of the proposed care and treatment. More recently, the Re. W case (*Re W (a minor) (medical treatment)*) held that the courts had jurisdiction to override a child's refusal to treatment where that refusal threatened the child's life (although the law on this is now not entirely clear). A child of any age may be given access to his health records if the record holder is satisfied that he is capable of understanding the nature of the application.

End of Compulsory Education

2.5   End of compulsory education (minimum school leaving age - MSLA) is generally around the child's 16th birthday.

2.6 Minimum School Leaving Age is defined as follows; "A child whose 16th birthday occurs between the 1st September and the 31st January (both dates inclusive) shall be deemed to be of compulsory school age until the end of the spring term which includes such month of January.

2.7 A child whose 16th birthday occurs between the 1st February and the 31st August (both dates inclusive) shall be deemed to be of compulsory school age until the Friday before the last Monday in May in that year".

2.8 In Northern Ireland, the upper limit of compulsory school age is reached

   i   for a person who attains the age of sixteen years between 1 September in any year and 1 July in the following year (both dates inclusive), on 30 June in that following year,

   ii   for a person who attains the age of sixteen years between 2 July and 31 August in any year (both dates inclusive), on 30 June in the following year.

Part-time employment

2.9 Generally 13 is the minimum age at which a child may have a part-time job, subject to various restrictions - see comments on Article 32.

Full time employment

2.10 Full time employment is permitted for those above minimum school leaving age - See 2.5-2.8 above.

Hazardous employment

2.11 Most health and safety legislation is not age specific and the Health and Safety Executive and local authority inspectors enforce it irrespective of the age of the employee. There are some substances, machines or processes (examples are lead, ionising radiation, woodworking machines) which pose a specific risk to the health and safety of young people. In these cases regulations generally prevent young people under 18 from doing the activity.

Sexual consent

2.12 In England, Scotland and Wales, a young person aged 16 can consent to sexual intercourse. In Northern Ireland, at 17 years of age, a young person may consent to sexual intercourse. A man will not be guilty of a charge of gross indecency with another man if both parties have reached the age of 21, although Parliament has recently voted to reduce the age to 18.

Marriage

2.13   In England and Wales, 16, with parental consent. If parental consent is refused, a court may authorise the marriage. Getting married between the ages of 16 and 18 without parental consent or permission of a court does not invalidate the marriage but it is a criminal offence. In Northern Ireland similar provisions apply. In Scotland a marriage can be contracted at age 16 without parental consent.

Voluntary enlistment in Armed Forces

2.14   The minimum age for enlistment is 16, where parental consent is granted. At 18 no parental consent is required to join the armed forces.

Conscription into the armed forces

2.15   All members of the British Armed Forces are volunteers.

Voluntarily giving evidence in court

2.16   A child of any age may give evidence in civil or criminal court proceedings. If the court decides that the child does not understand the nature of the oath he may give unsworn evidence provided that the court believes the child understands the duty to tell the truth.

Criminal Liability

2.17   In England and Wales a child between the ages of 10 and 13 (inclusive) can only be convicted of a criminal offence if it is proved that he or she knew what they were doing was wrong.

2.18   The Sexual Offences Act 1993 came into force on 20 September 1993 and this removed a previous assumption that a boy under 14 is incapable of sexual intercourse. A boy under 14 can now be charged and convicted of rape, assault with intent to commit rape, buggery and unlawful sexual intercourse with a girl under 16 etc.

2.19   At 14 also young people of both sexes can be sentenced to detention for "grave crimes" (punishable in adults with 14 or more years imprisonment). The Secretary of State decides where they will be placed. At 18 young people are dealt with in the adult rather than a juvenile court.

2.20   In Scotland the age of criminal liability is 8. Children between the ages of 8 and 16 who commit an offence would be referred to a children's hearing: over 16 they would be referred to an adult court. In the case of a major crime or one committed in the company of adults the child would be referred to the adult court. Children convicted in court of the gravest offences are placed in secure child care establishments.

2.21 In Northern Ireland, no child under the age of 10 can be guilty of any offence. Where a child is aged between 10 and 14 he may be charged with a crime provided the prosecution can prove that he knew what he was doing was wrong.

Deprivation of Liberty/ Imprisonment

2.22 A boy may qualify for a custodial sentence or be sentenced to detention in a young offender institution. At the age of 15 a young person who has committed an imprisonable offence may qualify for a custodial sentence but only in certain specified circumstances. If they receive a custodial sentence they will be sentenced to detention in a young offender institution. At 16 a child convicted of an imprisonable offence may be given a community service order. At 17 a probation order can be made. In Scotland a 16 year old may be given a custodial sentence in a young offenders institution; equally, the young person may be subject to non-custodial disposals (eg a community service order) which are increasingly used.

Consumption of alcohol

2.23 Drinking alcohol in private - 5. Admission to public house, but not to consume alcohol - 14. Drinking beer, wine or cider with a meal in a restaurant and purchasing liqueur chocolates - 16. Buying or drinking alcohol in a bar or public house - 18. In Scotland and Northern Ireland the law aims to prevent any person under the age of 18 from drinking alcohol in licensed premises. A person under the age of 18 must not purchase alcohol and must not consume it in any place other than a private residence. The holder of a licence in relation to licensed premises will be guilty of an offence if he permits a person under the age of 18 to be in any part of licensed premises during the hours when drinking alcohol is permitted.

Chapter 3: General Principles

Non discrimination - Article 2

3.1   Many countries have a written constitution enshrining certain rights and freedoms for the individual. However, under the United Kingdom's unwritten constitution, rights and freedoms are an inherent part of being a member of our society.

3.2   The UK Government does take specific steps to protect the rights and freedoms of individuals or groups of people if it considers such action is necessary. Our anti-discrimination legislation, principally the Sex Discrimination Act 1975 and the Race Relations Act 1976, prohibits discrimination against an individual on grounds of colour, race, nationality and sex.

3.3   The Children Act requires local authorities in the provision of services to families to have regard to a child's religious persuasion, racial origin and cultural and linguistic backgrounds. They are also required to take into account the different racial groups of children in their area when recruiting foster parents or arranging the provision of day care. Staff in children's homes should receive written guidance on important procedures which , dependent on the nature of the home, may include guidance on the particular care needs of children from minority ethnic groups and practices within the home to combat racism. Those responsible for recruiting staff to children's homes should seek to ensure that the composition of the staff group reflects the racial, cultural and linguistic background of the children being cared for and that there should be a proper balance between male and female staff.

Northern Ireland

3.4   It was recognised that in Northern Ireland with its two distinct religious groupings special measures were needed to tackle discrimination. Targeting Social Need, which is one of the main Public Expenditure priorities in Northern Ireland, aims to reduce unfair social and economic differentials between the 2 main religious groupings by ensuring that resources are targeted more effectively on the areas and people in greatest need. Employment and employability are priority areas for action.

3.5   The Central Community Relations Unit in Northern Ireland was established in 1987 following a recommendation of the Standing Advisory Commission on Human Rights. The Unit is charged with formulating, reviewing and challenging Government policy in order to address issues of equity and equality and improve community relations.

3.6   The Unit is undertaking a review of the effectiveness of the Fair Employment (Northern Ireland) Act 1989 and of progress towards equality of opportunity and fair participation in employment. The review, which is very wide-ranging, will include examination of the employment position of young persons from the 2 major religious blocs. Work is ongoing with a view to producing a report and recommendations by the end of 1995.

3.7   The Unit is also taking forward the Policy Appraisal and Fair Treatment initiative, which was launched by the Ministerial Group on Women's Issues. This has involved the development of guidance for all Departments of the Northern Ireland Civil Service and the Northern Ireland Office, designed to ensure that in relation to selected groups, consideration of equality, equity and non-discrimination are built from the outset to the preparation of policy proposals, including legislation, other initiatives and strategic plans for the implementation of policy and the delivery of services. Groups covered by the guidelines include:

i   people of different religious beliefs or political opinion;

ii   people of different gender;

iii   married and unmarried people;

iv   people with or without dependants;

v   people of different ethnic groups;

vi   people with or without a disability;

vii   people of different ages; and

viii people of different sexual orientation.

3.8   The Government is considering the scope of legislation to outlaw racial discrimination in Northern Ireland and what other steps might be taken to promote equality and equity for ethnic minorities there.

3.9   Under the Department of Health and Social Services' current Regional Strategy, Health and Social Services Boards are expected to identify areas and groups with particular needs and ensure that services (including those for children) are targeted accordingly. Boards are also expected to identify and seek to remove organisational or social barriers to services for disadvantaged groups.

3.10 One of the key elements of the proposed Children (Northern Ireland) Order will be that Boards will be required to have regard to a child's religious persuasion, racial origin and cultural and linguistic backgrounds in the provision of services. This is similar to the requirement on local authorities

19

in England and Wales under the Children Act.

3.11   As regards the rights of illegitimate children, the Order will reform the law on illegitimacy, reflecting changes made in England and Wales by the Family Law Reform Act 1987.   It will remove most of the legal disadvantages associated with birth outside marriage, mainly in relation to succession and property rights.   Consequently, the term "illegitimacy" will be given much less currency in the law and where it is thought necessary to draw a distinction, references will be made to children whose parents were not married to each other at the time of their birth.

3.12   The spirit of this Article permeates all aspects of the criminal justice system in Northern Ireland.

Provision of education

3.13   The Education Act 1944, as amended by the Education Act 1980, places local education authorities (LEAs) in England and Wales under a duty to make education available for all school-age children in their area, appropriate to their age, abilities and aptitudes.   This duty extends to all children residing in their area, whether permanently or temporarily and includes the children of displaced persons. The Education (Scotland) Act 1980 places similar duties on Scottish education authorities.

3.14   The Race Relations Act (RRA) 1976 applies to educational institutions, and the Secretary of State for Education and the Secretary of State for Scotland have specific powers in relation to complaints under the Race Relations Act about public sector institutions and local education authorities.

3.15   The RRA provides that a complainant alleging discrimination in the public sector of education must notify the Secretary of State of the complaint before initiating civil proceedings. In England and Wales the Secretary of State has powers to give directions (under Sections 68 and 99 of the Education Act 1944, as applied by Section 19 of the RRA) in any case brought to his notice where he considers that the requirements of the RRA have not been met.

3.16   Admission policies for schools and establishments in the further and higher education sectors must not discriminate against applicants on the grounds of race, colour, nationality or ethnic or national origin.

3.17   All local education authorities and governing bodies of voluntary-aided and self-governing state schools in England and Wales have been sent copies of a new Admissions Circular (issued in July 1993), which reminds schools of this requirement. Schools are already required to publish booklets every year including details of the number of pupils they plan to admit and how they will decide between applicants in the event of oversubscription.

Schools may, where appropriate, publish these booklets in local community languages.

3.18 Ethnic monitoring of school pupils in England and Wales was introduced in the 1990-91 academic year with the purpose of ensuring that the education provided in schools meets the needs of all pupils irrespective of their ethnic background. Local education authorities and self-governing (grant-maintained) schools are required to seek from parents, on a voluntary basis, information on their child's ethnic origin, mother tongue and religious affiliation. Data are being collected on each year's entry cohort to primary and secondary education. It will therefore take several years to build up a full profile of the school population. Unfortunately, the response so far has been poor and the survey is being kept under review. In Scotland, ethnic monitoring was included as a part of the School Census in 1989, collecting similar information as in England and Wales, but at entry to primary and secondary stages. Collection of information was suspended in 1992, with a view to improving response rates, and was restarted in 1993.

3.19 In England and Wales under Section 11 of the Local Government Act 1966 a grant is paid to local authorities (and other institutions) for the employment of additional staff to meet the particular needs of individuals arising from language and cultural barriers that inhibit access to mainstream provision and services. In 1993-94 central government grant for section 11 projects is £130.8m of which some 89% supports educational projects, involving some 8,800 full-time equivalent posts. Provision in 1994/95 is £110.7m. A recent change in the law has extended the scope of section 11 grant so that it may be paid to address the needs of any ethnic minority and not simply ethnic minority people of New Commonwealth origin. A similar provision is contained in the Local Government (Scotland) Act 1966.

3.20 Both the LEA maintained and grant-maintained sectors include a wide variety of schools of diverse religious denominations and faiths. In England and Wales the new Education Act 1993 increases the opportunities available for religious organisations to gain state funding for denominational schools. There are a number of denominational schools in the independent sector.

3.21 Sex discrimination is illegal under the terms of the Sex Discrimination Act 1975.

Best interests of the child - Article 3

3.22 In some of the areas which affect children's lives very significantly , for example health and education, there is an implicit acceptance in the system of the best interest principle although the there is no reference to it as such in the relevant legislation.

The Children Act 1989

3.23 Other Acts do, however, contain very specific references to the principle. The opening section of the Children Act 1989, which governs the care and upbringing of children in England and Wales sets out very explicitly the best interests principle. When courts are making decisions about the upbringing of children the welfare of the child is to be their paramount consideration. In many private law proceedings a court welfare officer will be appointed. He will report to the court on what is in the child's best interests. Courts are not to make any orders unless they are satisfied that making an order would be better for the child than making no order. They must also have regard to the principle that delay is likely to be prejudicial to the child's welfare. Courts may make a care or supervision order only if they are satisfied the child concerned is suffering or is likely to suffer significant harm. The same criteria have to be made out for the making of an Emergency Protection order or a Child Assessment Order and before a child can be taken into police protection. In public law proceedings the courts are required to appoint a guardian ad litem for the child unless satisfied that it is not necessary to do so in order to safeguard his interests. The guardian is under a duty to safeguard the child's interests. Courts can make orders restricting a child's liberty in non-criminal cases only if they are satisfied it is necessary to prevent him from suffering significant harm.

3.24 The Act places a duty on every local authority in England and Wales to safeguard and promote the welfare of children within their area who are in need. Where local authorities look after children the Act places a duty on the authority to safeguard and promote the child's best interests. Where a child is being looked after by a local authority they are required to advise and assist the child with a view to promoting his welfare when he ceases to be looked after by the authority. The only grounds on which local authorities are allowed to restrict contact between a child and his parents without a court order when the authority is looking after a child is that to allow contact would be contrary to the child's best interests.

3.25 Authorities are to appoint independent visitors for children being looked after who have little contact with their families but only if it would be in the child's best interests for this to happen. Where a child is accommodated in a voluntary or registered children's home the Act places the voluntary organisation and those carrying on the registered home under a duty to safeguard and promote the child's welfare. Local authorities are required to satisfy themselves that these bodies are carrying out their duties. Local authorities are required to visit such children in the interests of their welfare and to take action if they are not satisfied that a child's welfare is being safeguarded. They have a similar duty in respect of children who are being privately fostered. Local authorities have the power to prohibit a person from being a private foster parent if they believe it would be prejudicial to the welfare of the child for him to be accommodated by that person.

3.26 Local authorities were given new duties to promote the welfare of children accommodated by a health authority or local education authority, children accommodated in residential care, nursing or mental nursing homes and in independent schools. Proprietors of independent schools are required to safeguard and promote the welfare of boarders and local authorities are required to ensure proprietors are carrying out this duty.

3.27 The Children Act recognises that primarily responsibility for the upbringing of children rests with parents. Where parents are experiencing difficulties in this task local authorities are to assist them through the provision of services delivered in a non stigmatising fashion. In cases where the provision of services does not prove sufficient to ensure children are not placed in jeopardy local authorities have power to take effective protective action within a framework of proper safeguards of parents' rights and responsibilities. The Act introduced two new orders, the Child Assessment Order and the Emergency Protection Order aimed at safeguarding children's welfare.

3.28 The best interests principle is contained not only in the Act itself but is a theme which runs through the regulations made under the Act, and the accompanying guidance.

Best interests of the child in Northern Ireland and Scotland

3.29 The proposed Children (Northern Ireland) Order will make the welfare of the child the first consideration in any decision affecting his or her care and upbringing.

3.30 At present, when making decisions in relation to custody or access, courts must regard the welfare of the child as the first and paramount consideration. This is recognised as an established principle of common law. This will assume greater importance when the proposed Children (Northern Ireland) Order is enacted and the position in Northern Ireland will be similar to that in England and Wales under the Children Act 1989. Under the Order, where a court determines any question in respect of a child's upbringing or the administration of a child's property, the child's welfare should be the court's primary consideration. Courts must also have regard to the supplementary principles that delay in proceedings relating to a child's upbringing would be prejudicial to a child's welfare and that an order should not be made with respect to a child unless it would be better for the child to make the order than to make no order at all. The Order will contain a checklist of factors to which a court must have regard when considering the child's welfare.

3.31 The Child Support (NI) Order 1991 provides that the welfare of the child must be taken into account when exercising any discretionary powers under that Order.

3.32 In the Social Work (Scotland) Act 1968 the best interests of the child are established as central to any decisions on the care of a child, whether under voluntary arrangements or by compulsory measures of care. Children's hearings in deciding on compulsory measures are required to consider the best interests of the child.

Day Care

3.33 Day care services used by young children have been subject to statutory regulation by local authorities since 1948. New provisions in the Children Act retained the legal framework of applicants for registration as providers of day care being considered "fit" to look after young children,but made this concept simpler to operate. The Department of Health issued general guidance on the new legislation in 1991, with a further circular put out in January 1993. The Welsh Office issued a similar circular in March. This made it clear that the purpose of registration with the local authority is: to protect children; to provide some reassurance to parents,who are asking someone else to look after their child, who is vulnerable by virtue of his age,in their absence; to ensure that independent services and child minders maintain acceptable standards. The guidance included recommendations on staffing levels and space standards as well as material on good practice issues such as factors known to influence the quality of care.

Police checks and vetting of staff working with children

3.34 In addition to normal recruitment procedures local authorities have ,since 1986, been able to undertake checks with the police on the possible criminal background of those they wish to employ to work with children. These police vetting arrangements were extended to staff working with children in the National Health Service in 1988. Revised guidance reminding authorities of these arrangements, and clarifying the circumstances in which they should be used, was issued in October 1993.

3.35 In August 1989 the Government set up three pilot schemes which allowed participating voluntary organisations to undertake police checks on staff and volunteers working with children. In the light of the experience of the pilot studies, a national scheme (covering all the major national children's charities) has remained in operation and, since October 1993, its scope has been extended to embrace staff working in all voluntary children's homes. The Government also sponsored the production of a code of practice for safeguarding the welfare of children for voluntary organisations in England and Wales. It was published in October 1993.

3.36 The Department of Health has, for many years, offered a Consultancy service to those proposing to engage staff and volunteers to work with children. Checks may be made against a list of people drawn to the attention of the Department who have ceased to be engaged in working with children in circumstances where the welfare of children has been, or was likely to be, put at risk. The purpose of the Service is to ensure appropriate references are taken up, by putting those considering offering employment in the child care field in touch with relevant past employers.

3.37 The Disqualification for Caring for Children Regulations are a further safeguard for children being cared for outside the family setting. They apply to any person wishing to be a private foster parent, a child minder, a day care provider or to run a voluntary or private children's home. The Regulations prohibit persons from carrying out any of these roles if:

i   they have previously been convicted of certain offences or

ii   if a child of theirs has been the subject of care proceedings or has been removed from their care or prevented from living with them or

iii   where they have been refused registration as a child minder or day care provider or have been removed from the register or

iv   have been refused registration to run a private or voluntary home or have been concerned with a private or voluntary home which has been removed from the register or

v   have been prohibited from being a private foster parent.

3.38 There is a discretionary power to lift the disqualification but this is to be used in exceptional circumstances and after the most careful consideration.

3.39 The best interests principle is also found in the juvenile justice system. A central principle of the Children and Young Persons Act 1933 is that in disposing of the case a court must have regard to the welfare of the young person.

Health and Safety

3.40 The Health and Safety at Work Act 1974 (HSWA) section 3 lays a duty on an employer "to conduct his undertaking in such a way as to ensure, so far as is reasonably practicable, that persons not in his employment who may be affected thereby are not thereby exposed to risks to their health or safety". This means those responsible for children's homes, educational establishments or child minding must run their business in a safe and healthy way. Health and Safety Executive (HSE) inspectors enforce the Act and associated legislation in these areas, including home-based child minders. Children play on farms, building sites and even railway tracks and much of HSE's work concerning children is concentrated on ensuring employers take practical steps to keep inquisitive and vulnerable children out of these potentially dangerous places.

3.41   The Management of Health and Safety Regulations, which came into force on 1 January 1993, ensure that employers introduce arrangements for planning, organising, controlling, monitoring and reviewing their management of health and safety : all schools must now have a health and safety policy. The Health and Safety Executive's Inspectorate have powers to ensure that schools comply with the requirements of the HSW Act.

3.42   The Education (School Premises) Regulations 1981 place certain obligations on employers which relate, among other things, to the structure and fabric of the buildings and the means of escape in the event of fire. The current Regulations include a general requirement that the health and safety of the occupants of a school building are "reasonably assured".

3.43   The Department for Education, Scottish Office Education Department and the Health and Safety Commission provide guidance to schools on health and safety.

3.44   Education Regulations require that at schools and further education institutions the staff employed should be suitable and sufficient in numbers. The Secretary of State for Education has powers to bar the employment of persons in schools on medical grounds or grounds of misconduct.

The right to life, survival and development - Article 6

3.45   The UK fully accepts that every child has the inherent right to life.

3.46   The Health Service in the UK is open to all, regardless of income, largely free at the point of delivery. All health service patients must be treated free of charge unless there is a specific power to charge - for example, for prescriptions. Children under 16 are exempt from paying for prescriptions.

3.47   The most significant factor in promoting children's survival in the UK has been the success of our child immunisation programme. The infant mortality rate has been halved between 1978 and 1992. The halving of the rate of Sudden Infant Death Syndrome between 1991 and 1992 is also a considerable achievement.

3.48   Considerable progress has been made in reducing accidental deaths in children and young people. In the year to June 1993 a reduction of 15 % has been achieved in child road accident casualties compared with the 1981-85 baseline average.

3.49   There has also been encouraging progress in our understanding of child development as a result of advances across disciplines like paediatrics, neurology and psychology. These have enabled earlier diagnosis of physical and sensory impairments in children and the arrangement of therapeutic programmes intended to minimise their impact on the growth and development of the child.

3.50   All children aged 0-5 years have a named health visitor who offers a universal service of support and advice on child rearing matters. The type of services provided are checks on health and development, screening tests, advice on diet and accident prevention etc. The service also provides an opportunity to identify children in need, as defined by the Children Act, and a link to be made with Social Services if required.

3.51   All of these issues are dealt with in greater detail in Chapter 6 - Basic Health and Welfare.

Respect for the views of the child - Article 12

The Children Act

3.52   A central principle of the Children Act, which applies in England and Wales is that the voice of the child must be heard. When a court determines a question about the upbringing of a child they have to have regard in particular to the ascertainable wishes and feelings of the child. The Act allows children for the first time, if they obtain the leave of the court, to apply in their own right for certain orders.

3.53   In many private law proceedings a court welfare officer or the Official Solicitor will be appointed. One of his duties is to ascertain the wishes and feelings of the child and convey these to the court.

3.54   In most public law proceedings a guardian ad litem will be appointed for the child. One of the guardian's specific tasks under the Court Rules is to report to the court on the wishes of the child in respect of matters relating to the proceedings. If the child is capable of instructing his solicitor direct he may do so separately from the guardian.

3.55   When courts make a child assessment or an emergency protection order or an interim care or supervision order they can attach a direction to them about a medical or psychiatric examination of the child. If, however, the child is of sufficient age and understanding to make an informed decision he can refuse to submit to the examination.

3.56   When local authorities are making decisions about children whom they are looking after the Children Act requires them to take account of the children's wishes and feelings. They are required under regulations to tell children what plans they have made about their placement. Before conducting reviews of these arrangements they have to seek and take into account the wishes of the children. The Department of Health's formal guidance makes clear that the child's attendance at the review should be the norm not the exception. He should not however be required to attend against his wishes.

3.57 The same principle applies to the participation of children in child protection conferences, which are held to decide whether the child is at risk of abuse and whether his or her name should be placed on a local Child Protection Register. Whenever children have sufficient understanding and are able to express their wishes and feelings and to participate in the process of investigation, assessment, planning and review, they should be encouraged to attend conferences. This is clearly set out in the Government guidance "Working Together" on inter-agency co-operation for the protection of children from abuse.

3.58 Children who are dissatisfied with the care they are receiving have the right themselves to access the local authority's complaints procedure. Regulations require local authorities to set up a representations procedure with an independent element to consider complaints and other representations made by children, parents or others with a legitimate interest in the child, in relation to the local authority's discharge of its family support functions. Voluntary organisations and registered children's homes are required to set up similar procedures for representations or complaints by or on the behalf of children accommodated by them.

3.59 The guidance on the conduct of children's homes emphasises the need to take into account the wishes of the children in the home in the day to day running of the home. No independent visitor can be appointed for a child unless the child consents.

3.60 In Scotland the child is fully involved in proceedings before children's hearings and is encouraged to participate fully in the discussions which precede decisions on whether compulsory measures of care are required and if so, what form they should take. Local Authorities are urged to take full account of the views of the child in considering or reviewing programmes of care.

Education

3.61 In the field of education in England and Wales, there is no obstacle in law to prevent children themselves from making a complaint, either

    i   under section 23 of the Education Reform Act 1988 about the actions of Local Education Authorities (LEAs) or governing bodies relating to the curriculum or religious worship in schools; or

ii   under sections 68 and 99 of the Education Act 1944, as amended by section 219 of the Education Reform Act 1988, to the Secretary of State about the conduct of an LEA or a school governing body.

3.62   Similarly in Scotland, complaints may be made by children against an education authority, a School Board or other person for failing to discharge any of their educational duties, to the Secretary of State under section 70 of the Education (Scotland) Act 1980.

3.63   Procedures relating to exclusion from school are laid down in the Education (No.2) Act 1986, as amended by the Education Act 1993. Under the general law, a head teacher must allow a pupil an opportunity to make representations either personally or through a representative before taking a decision to exclude a pupil. In addition, the 1986 Act provides for formal appeals (in the case of permanent exclusions) to be lodged by parents and the pupil himself if over 18 and specifically requires the appellant to be given an opportunity to make representations. The Government has recently conducted a review of exclusion procedures and practice and the Department for Education will be issuing in May 1994 guidance on exclusion policy and practice. One of the issues to be addressed will be involvement of the child. In Scotland exclusion procedures are set out in the Education (Scotland) Act 1986. Regulations confer on the child rights to appeal to the education authority appeals committee, then to the Sheriff court.

3.64   The Education Act 1993 provides for the establishment of a Special Educational Needs Tribunal to consider appeals by parents against decisions by LEAs concerning their children's special educational needs. In reaching its decisions the Tribunal will have a statutory duty to have regard to the Code of Practice. That code will enshrine the need for LEAs to consult with pupils before reaching decisions on their needs.

3.65   Consistently with Article 18.1, parents have a legal duty to ensure that their children receive an education. It follows that it is the parents' preference which is considered by admissions authorities when school places are allocated. It is not expected that parents will reach their decision without taking their child's wishes into account but, as the duty to ensure that child is educated falls to the parents, the right to express a preference for the school at which that education will take place should also fall to the parent.

3.66   If parents do not receive their choice of school, they have the right to an appeal before an independent committee. If this committee rules in favour of the parents, the child must be admitted to the school. Parents applying for places at LEA maintained schools also have the right to complain to the Local Government Ombudsman if they are dissatisfied with the appeals process. The Education Act 1993 will extend the Ombudsman's power to cover aided, special agreement and Grant-Maintained schools.

Appeals against Records of Needs are decided by the Secretary of State in Scotland; appeals against schools specific in the Records are taken by the education authority's appeals committee.

Broadcasting

3.67 The Broadcasting Standards Council (BSC) was established to consider the public's views on television programmes and to consider complaints relating to matters of taste and decency. The BSC have conducted research into the views of schoolchildren (sixth formers), and will consider complaints from children. The BSC has published research working papers on "Children, Television and Morality" and the "Future of Children's Television in Britain" amongst others. Further research into the way children in the 6-16 age group cope with frightening material on television, the peer pressure to watch this sort of material and the ways in which parents regulate television viewing is underway at present. The Broadcasting Complaints Commission (BCC) was set up to investigate complaints of misrepresentation by television programmes of individuals. The BCC will consider complaints received from children, and have allowed a child to be represented in these administrative procedures. Both the BCC and BSC fund the complaints process for all complainants.

Northern Ireland

3.68 At present in Northern Ireland there is not a developed jurisprudence in relation to ensuring that the views of the child are given weight in all matters affecting him. The child's views are currently expressed through the medium of a welfare report, and the older the child, the greater the weight to be attached to his opinion.

3.69 Under the proposed Children (Northern Ireland) Order, which will seek to ensure that the views of children are taken into account in any decisions affecting them, this will assume greater prominence, since courts (in both public and private proceedings) and Health and Social Services Boards will be required to take into account the views of the child (in the light of his age and understanding) when applying the welfare principle.

3.70 The child's views will also be put before the court through representation by a guardian and litem as in England and Wales.

3.71 In private law proceedings, provision will be made to enable the child, with the leave of the court, to be made a party to proceedings in respect of, for example, a residence order or a prohibited steps order.

3.72 Under current procedures, Health and Social Services Boards encourage children in care who have sufficient understanding to be involved in decisions about themselves. Parents are welcome to participate at case conferences. Complaints and grievance procedures for children in residential and non-residential care ensure that there are means of redress for grievances.

3.73 This Article has relevance for all areas of criminal justice including police interviews, court hearings and internal Training School procedures and the issues involved are being looked at.

Chapter 4: Civil Rights and Freedoms

Name and Nationality - Article 7

Name

4.1   The Birth and Death Registration Act 1953 lays down that all births in England and Wales must be registered in the sub-district in which they occur. The surname given at registration can be the mother's, father's, a combination of both or a completely different surname. The name recorded in the register should be the surname in which it is intended to bring the child up in. There is no facility to change the surname in the register at a later date unless it can be proved that an error was made at the time of registration. However it is possible to change a surname by common usage, statutory declaration or deed poll although such changes would not be recorded in the register.

4.2   In Northern Ireland, by virtue of the Births and Deaths Registration (Northern Ireland) Order 1976, the birth of every child must be registered. In respect of legitimate children, both the father and the mother are under a duty to register the birth. A child born to married parents will generally take his father's surname, however a child whose parents are not married normally takes his mother's surname. A young child has no power to change his name although both his parents acting in agreement may do so. Where the parents of a child are not married to each other, the inclusion of the father's name in the register of births is prima facie evidence of his paternity and for this reason a different procedure is used for the entry of the father's name on the register. Accordingly, the father's name may only be entered on the register at the joint request of both parents who sign the register in the presence of each other, or at the request of the mother alone, on production of a formal declaration by herself, stating that the person is the father of the child and also a formal declaration made by that person acknowledging that he is the father of the child.

Nationality - Children born in the UK

4.3   A child born in the United Kingdom to a parent who is a British Citizen or settled in the UK acquires British citizenship automatically. A child born in the UK who does not become a British citizen at birth is entitled to be registered as such if one of his parents becomes a British citizen or becomes settled in the UK. Failing that a child has an entitlement to registration once he reaches the age of 10 if he has spent no more than 90 days outside the United Kingdom in each year of his life. There is also a provision for <u>any</u> minor to be registered as a British citizen at the discretion of the Secretary of State.

Nationality - Children born overseas

4.4   A person born outside the United Kingdom will acquire British citizenship by descent if either of his parents is a British citizen <u>otherwise than by descent</u> (ie having acquired it by birth, adoption, registration or naturalisation in the United Kingdom). He will acquire citizenship by descent if either parent is a British citizen and at the time of birth is in Crown service, service under a European Community institution, or in service which the Secretary of State has designated as being closely associated with the activities outside the United Kingdom of Her Majesty's Government in the UK. In addition, there is an entitlement to registration as British citizens for other children born abroad to parents who are British citizens by descent and who spend a large part of their lives outside the United Kingdom.

Nationality - Children born stateless

4.5   Schedule 2 of the British Nationality Act 1981 was introduced to facilitate United Kingdom compliance with the United Nations Convention on the Reduction of Statelessness. It contains various provisions entitling those born stateless both before and after 1 January 1983 (the date on which the 1981 Act came into effect) either in the United Kingdom, a dependent territory or elsewhere, to acquire the status of British citizen, British Dependent Territories citizen, British Overseas citizen or British Subject. In practice most children will acquire citizenship of their parents' country of origin. The United Kingdom does not however recognise a right for a stateless child to acquire British citizenship automatically if born here.

Reservation on Immigration and Nationality

4.6   The UK's immigration and nationality law is entirely consistent with the thrust of the Convention. The Convention was drafted in fairly general terms in respect of immigration and nationality, and therefore, to avoid endless argument about the extent to which the detail of immigration and nationality law is in keeping with the letter and spirit of these generalised statements, an omnibus reservation was entered making it clear that nothing in the Convention will be interpreted as overriding the operation of UK immigration and nationality legislation.

Preservation of identity - Article 8

Name

4.7   Under the Children Act in England and Wales, and the proposed Children (Northern Ireland) Order it is a condition of all residence orders (a residence order under the Children Act is a court order determining with which of two separated parents or other relative a child will live) that no person may cause the child to be known by a new surname without either the written consent of every person who has parental responsibility, or the leave of the court. Consequently, although it may be in a child's interests to have his name changed, it is recognised that a child's surname is an important symbol of his identity and his relationship with his parents. It is, therefore, not a matter on which a parent with whom the child lives should be able to take unilateral action. Where both parents are in agreement and wish to change the child's surname and the child objects to the change, he can seek leave to apply to a court for a prohibited steps order under the Children Act in England and Wales which, if granted, would prevent his name being changed. The position in Northern Ireland will be same when the Children (Northern Ireland) order comes into force. While a child is the subject of a care order no person may cause the child to be known by a new surname without either the written consent of every person who has parental responsibility or the leave of the court.

4.8   Where the issue of changing a child's surname comes before a court, it must treat the child's welfare as its paramount consideration. It is anticipated that courts will continue to regard the change of a child's surname as an important matter.

4.9   There is no statutory provision in Scottish Law directly relating to names of children. However, the exercise of parental rights under the Law Reform (Parent and Child) (Scotland) Act 1986 makes provision for the exercise of parental rights which could include the giving or changing of a child's name. Any person claiming an interest (which could include the child) may apply to the court for an order relating to such rights. If such an application is made, the court has the power to resolve disputes over an aspect of a child's upbringing, including the changing of a name. As in England and Wales, the court must regard the welfare of the child as the paramount consideration.

Nationality

4.10 A child may only be deprived of British nationality in certain circumstances. If he acquired his citizenship by birth or adoption he cannot be deprived of it. He must have been registered. The citizenship must then have been acquired by fraud, false representation or concealment of any material fact. (Citizenship can also be removed on grounds of disloyalty towards Her Majesty the Queen, or the imposition of a prison sentence of 12 months or more within 5 years of the date of registration, but these grounds are hardly likely to arise with children.) The process of deprivation is overseen by an independent committee of inquiry established under the terms of the statute.

4.11 The grant of citizenship may be null and void where, for instance, a registration involved deception as to the applicant's identity. This has been held by UK courts as suitable grounds for holding that there was no acquisition of citizenship from the start. Citizenship is not taken away: it never existed in the first place. In such cases no recourse is had to the deprivation machinery; the matter is dealt with administratively.

Freedom of expression, association and peaceful assembly - Articles 13 and 15

4.12 It is a fundamental principle of British law that citizens (including children) are entitled to do any act unless it is specifically proscribed. Therefore, children have the full rights set out in Articles 13, 14 and 15 and are subject only to the restrictions recognised as being necessary in the Convention in order to protect the rights of others.

Public Order

4.13 The principal statute governing public order is the Public Order Act 1986. This provides, inter alia:

i   Public order offences, ranging from riots down to behaviour likely to cause harassment, alarm or distress. These offences cover both insulting words and behaviour and the display of written material;

ii   provisions enabling chief officers of police to impose conditions on public processions and public assemblies in order to protect the community against serious public disorder or disruption and, in very tightly defined circumstances, to enable a local authority, with the Home Secretary's consent, to prohibit public processions (but not assemblies); and

iii   provisions to deter incitement to racial hatred.

4.14 All these provisions involve some restrictions on freedom of movement and/or expression but they are used only in circumstances which the Convention permits. Children above the age of criminal responsibility (10 in England and Wales) are subject to the provisions of these laws, as any others (though penalties might be lower than for adults).

Political Expression

4.15 Section 44 of the Education (No 2) Act 1986 requires local education authorities, school governing bodies and head teachers in England and Wales to forbid the pursuit of partisan political activities by pupils under age 12. It also requires them to forbid the promotion of partisan political views in any teaching at the school. Section 45 of the Act requires them to take such steps as are reasonably practicable to ensure that, where political issues are brought to pupils' attention, the pupils are offered a balanced presentation of opposing views.

4.16 These provisions aim to ensure that children, especially impressionable younger children, are not manipulated while at school.

4.17 The provisions, including the prohibition against partisan political activities by junior pupils, apply only at school or during out-of-school activities organised by the school. Children may do as they wish in their own time.

Freedom of thought, conscience and religion - Article 14

4.18 The United Kingdom has a long tradition of tolerance and the Government believes that no unnecessary obstacle should be placed in the way of people wishing to observe their own customs, religion and law.

4.19 Every person in the United Kingdom has the right to religious freedom, subject only to such limitations as are prescribed in law and are necessary for the protection of the rights and freedoms of others. They may manifest his or her faith in teaching, worship and observance without interference from the community or the state. There is no compulsory state religion. There is complete freedom of thought, conscience or form of worship. There is no restriction on the right of any citizen to change his or her religion.

4.20 Religious education and daily collective worship must be provided by all maintained schools in England and Wales for all registered pupils. Parents, however, have the right to withdraw their children from religious education and daily collective worship either in whole or in part.

4.21 Religious education syllabuses for county schools must be non-denominational. The Department for Education has advised local education authorities that religious education syllabuses should not be designed to convert pupils, or to urge a particular religion or religious belief on pupils. The content of the syllabus must mainly reflect Christianity, but it must also cover the other principal religions represented in Great Britain. Voluntary schools may provide denominational religious education, but parents may, if there is not a local county school, request that their children follow a county syllabus.

4.22 Collective worship in county schools must be organised having regard to the relevant circumstances relating to pupils' family backgrounds, their ages and aptitudes. Depending on these factors, it may be broadly Christian, either wholly or mainly, or non-Christian.

4.23 Students are not required to attend the religious education and collective worship provided at further education institutions.

4.24 At present, at common law in Northern Ireland, a minor cannot choose his own religion. Once the proposed Children (Northern Ireland) Order is enacted, the position in Northern Ireland will be similar to that in England and Wales under the Children Act 1989, and a person with parental responsibility will have the right to determine the child's religious education. Where a child is sufficiently mature to make his own determination, the provision, that a person with parental responsibility may choose a child's religion, must be read in conjunction with the "Gillick" decision, which established the principle that parental rights yield to the child's right to make his own decisions when he reaches a sufficient understanding and intelligence to be capable of making up his own mind on a matter.

4.25 Where a child is being looked after by a local authority the authority is required to have regard to the child's religious persuasion, racial origin and cultural and linguistic background when making decisions about him. Also the authority has to take into account the child's wishes and feelings. Children accommodated in children's homes are required by regulation to be given the opportunity to practise their religion. Positive steps are to be taken to facilitate their doing so.

Protection of Privacy - Article 16

4.26 United Kingdom law does not provide for a statutory right of privacy. Children are afforded the same protection as adults under the general law (for example the law on slander and libel, and on interference with correspondence, and the Data Protection Act 1984 which provides for safeguards against the misuse of computerised personal information).

4.27 Two recently published reports deal with privacy matters: an independent report of a review of press self-regulation; and a report by a Select Committee of the House of Commons on privacy and media intrusion. In the light of these reports, the Government is considering whether any further statutory measures may be needed to deal with intrusions into personal privacy.

4.28 Children's homes in England and Wales are required under the Children's Homes Regulations to provide suitable facilities to allow children to meet privately with their family and a range of other people.

4.29 Children's Homes are required by Regulations to have a telephone where children can make and receive telephone calls in private.

4.30 Homes are also required to consider how they might provide special privacy in which to allow a child to pursue his religion.

4.31   Residential child care practice in Northern Ireland promotes a homely living environment for children, which includes the rights of privacy, when required.

Access to appropriate information - Article 17

Media

4.32   The mass media in the United Kingdom are aware of the need to disseminate information and material of social and cultural benefit to children.   The Broadcasting Act 1990 makes it a requirement for Channel 3 companies to provide programming for children.   The Independent Television Commission (ITC) has specified that broadcasters must show at least 10 hours per week, consisting of a range of entertainment, drama and information programmes; these should include provision for children of pre-school age.   Channel 4 is required to broadcast schools programmes.   The BBC is committed to providing a wide range of high quality programmes for children, including drama, sitcoms, quiz shows, leisure and entertainment and news.   For example, 'Newsround' is a regular news and information programme specifically aimed at children.   BBC education programmes include school programmes broadcast for 30 weeks a year both on television and radio, which cover a full range of topics, such as drama, documentaries, comedy, music, poetry, animations and computer graphics.   Special provision is also made for music, dance and drama programmes for five to twelve year olds.

4.33   The British Film Institute (BFI) takes into account the needs of children in its activities.   Among other things, the BFI arranges programmes of children's films in London and elsewhere, advises on media education in the national curriculum, and provides film and television material for use in children's television programmes, both for entertainment and schools broadcasts. The Wales Film Council is partly funded by the BFI. Schools media education is promoted through funding partnerships with the Welsh Office and local authorities.

4.34   Under the Public Libraries and Museums Act 1964, local authorities have a statutory duty to provide a comprehensive library service for children as well as adults.   The Arts Council's literature department supports reading among children through support for the Arts Council Children's Literature Summer School and through its support for the Children's Book Foundation.

4.35   Minority indigenous linguistic needs are catered for by the requirement for the Welsh television company S4C to broadcast a substantial proportion of its programmes in the Welsh language, and by the funding (approximately

£10m) supplied to the Gaelic Television Committee for them to ensure that a wide range of high quality television programmes are available for broadcast in Gaelic in Scotland.

4.36 The broadcasting regulatory authorities, the BBC, the ITC and the Radio Authority (RA), have established clear guidelines and codes of practice to seek to ensure that children are protected from material which could harm their mental, moral or physical development. Television broadcasters apply a general 'watershed' at 9 pm (8pm for encrypted services) before which programmes must be suitable for a family audience including children.

4.37 Guidelines on children's programmes cover the areas of violence, language and general taste and decency. These guidelines take into account the context of the action and the danger of imitative behaviour by children. In the area of news and factual programmes there is particular awareness of a child's vulnerability and suggestibility. Broadcasters must also be aware of the dangers to children of programmes which include psychic or occult practices, smoking, drinking alcohol and drug taking.

4.38 The protection of children from unsuitable material on television is one of the primary functions of the BSC, and is an essential feature of the Council's Code of Practice. The Broadcasting Act 1990 imposes a duty on each broadcasting or regulatory body to reflect the Council's Code in their own guidelines.

4.39 The provision of educational broadcasting for schools is ensured under the Broadcasting Act 1990 and the BBC Charter. The output of the BBC and independent television networks is of a very high standard; is increasingly geared to the needs of the National Curriculum in England and Wales; and is well used and much appreciated by schools. Over 1000 hours per year of schools programmes are broadcast. Access to the output is facilitated by the Copyright, Designs and Patents Act 1988 and the Broadcasting Act 1990.

Sex Education

4.40 The Education Act 1993 requires all maintained secondary schools in England and Wales to provide sex education (including education about HIV and AIDS and other sexually transmitted diseases) for all their pupils. It remains at the discretion of individual governing bodies whether sex education is provided in maintained primary schools. The Act gives parents the right to withdraw their children from all or part of the sex education offered at school, which is in keeping with Articles 5 and 18.1 of the Convention. The biological aspects of human sexual reproduction remain within the National Curriculum, and as such remain compulsory for all pupils in maintained schools.

4.41 The Education Act 1993 does not apply in Scotland, and therefore

Scottish schools are not required by statute to provide sex education. Guidelines issued by the Scottish Office Education Department in 1993 give health education, including sex education a firm place in the curriculum and set out specific learning targets. There is no statutory right for parents to withdraw their children from sex education in Scotland. However the views of parents should be considered and they should be encouraged to discuss any reservations they have about particular aspects of the curriculum. Discussion can often remove difficulties or lead to satisfactory alternative arrangements being made. These may include the acceptance that the pupil will not attend certain classes, if that seems the best course.

The Children Act

4.42 In the case of the Children Act in England and Wales, the government perceived it was very important that children have rights of access to information on this major reform of legislation affecting them. Three booklets were produced by the Department of Health to explain to young people their rights under the Children Act.

The booklets were:

The Children Act and the Courts - A Guide for Young People

Getting Help from Social Services

Living Away from Home - Your Rights

4.43 The booklets aimed to ensure that children themselves understood what help and advice they can get and how to get it. They were written in a simple and straightforward style with colourful graphics. The booklets follow on from two booklets for parents and a leaflet for children on the Children Act issued previously.

4.44 The booklets were given a wide distribution to, amongst others; Social Services Departments; every older child or young person being looked after by a local authority; Voluntary Children's Homes; Voluntary Organisations; Public Libraries; Youth Centres and youth organisations.

4.45 The booklet produced to inform children and adults about this Convention has been mentioned earlier in this report.

Children's Reporters in Scotland

4.46 Children's Reporters in Scotland provide explanatory material for young people about the proceedings in which they will participate, before any decisions are taken on compulsory measures of care. In addition many local authorities provide written information on care programmes.

British Aid Programme

4.47 Under the British Aid Programme, the Overseas Development Administration's (ODA) social development advisers are involved in the development of materials of concern to children in conjunction with local people overseas. It is particularly important to encourage the local capacity to produce these materials. Careful attention is paid to them, to ensure that they reflect the local cultural diversity adequately.

The right not to be subjected to torture or other cruel, inhuman or degrading treatment or punishment - Article 37a

4.48 Section 134 of the Criminal Justice Act 1988, makes it an offence to torture a person in the circumstances described. The offence is punishable with a maximum of life imprisonment. The age of the victim is immaterial as is whether the pain or suffering is physical or mental and whether it is caused by an act or an omission.

4.49 Courts have no power to order any form of cruel or degrading treatment or punishment to young offenders.

4.50 Regulations made under the Children Act and the accompanying guidance have given effect to the government's policy that corporal punishment has no place in the child care setting. In addition, because of the special vulnerability of children in children's homes, Regulations also prohibit a range of other punishments in homes.

4.51 The regulations on children's homes in Scotland specifically exclude corporal punishment from the arrangements for discipline in such homes. Monitoring and inspection reports on residential child care in Northern Ireland indicate that no degrading forms of punishment of children are practised in children's homes.

Chapter 5: Family Environment and Alternative Care

Parental Guidance - Article 5

5.1   The Children Act recognises that in general parents are the best people to bring up their children. They retain parental responsibility even when their children no longer live with them. They lose responsibility only if the child is adopted.

5.2   Parental responsibility is defined as all the rights, duties, powers, responsibilities and authority which by law a parent of a child has in relation to the child and his property. It is recognised that as the child matures he will become increasingly capable of making his own decisions concerning his life. This philosophy was reflected in a court judgement, commonly known as the Gillick judgement. The court emphasised that parental rights to control children exist for the benefit of the child not the parent.

5.3   The right of parents to provide appropriate direction and guidance to children in the exercise of their right to education has been strengthened by recent developments in the statutory framework for education. Parents can now exercise increased choice and have more of a say in the running of schools.

5.4   Details of parents' rights and responsibilities have been disseminated to parents in The Parent's Charter published in September 1991. The Parent's Charter sets out clearly the rights, choices and responsibilities of parents concerning their children's education. A second edition of the Charter which will explain the main policy developments over the last two years, particularly those arising from the 1993 Education Act, is scheduled for publication in 1994.

Parental responsibilities - Article 18 paras 1-2

Parental responsibility and the law

5.5   One of several major changes to the private law relating to children that the Children Act introduces for England and Wales is the concept of parental responsibility. If parents were married to each other at the time of a child's birth , or if they have been married to each other at any time since the child's conception, they each have parental responsibility. Unmarried fathers do not have parental responsibility but can acquire it by means of an agreement with the mother or through a court order. It is a shared right and a shared duty throughout the child's life. If the parents separate or divorce that responsibility does not disappear nor is it reallocated to one parent rather than the other. It continues to be shared. It is lost only in adoption.

5.6   Where parents are experiencing difficulties in bringing up their children local authorities are to help them to do so by providing a range of services. The services are to be provided in partnership with the family, having taken account of their wishes. They are to be provided in a non stigmatising fashion.

5.7   In Scotland it is intended to amend existing legislation to define parental responsibilities and rights and to introduce other changes in the light of the recommendations of the Scottish Law Commission's Report on Family Law.

5.8   The Children (Northern Ireland) Order emphasises parental responsibility for bringing up children, while ensuring that the statutory agencies are there to help when needed and will seek to reduce the level of compulsory intervention in family life. The Order will also seek to encourage greater partnership between parents and the statutory service and greater use of voluntary arrangements, rather than statutory intervention.

5.9   When a child offends against the criminal law, the parent's responsibility for their child's offending behaviour is brought home through a number of measures aimed at ensuring the parents attend court with their child, providing for parents to pay any fines or compensation order imposed on the child where appropriate, and providing for parents to be bound over to ensure their child's good behaviour. There are plans to introduce measures to ensure parents co-operate with any community sentence imposed on their child.

Duty to educate children

5.10   Parents have a legal duty under the Education Acts to ensure that their children receive an education.

Financial Support

5.11   The Child Support Act 1991, which came into force from April 1993, is designed to ensure that both parents fulfil their financial obligations towards their children, irrespective of what has happened to their own relationship. Levels of maintenance are based on a formula which is fair and consistent and also takes account of the needs of any children of a new partnership. The Child Support Agency provides a fast, efficient service and ensures that, where necessary, appropriate enforcement action is taken. There is a separate Child Support Agency in Northern Ireland. The relevant legislation there is the Child Support (Northern Ireland) Order 1991. In the case of children living in Scotland, the Child Support Act 1991 empowers a child aged 12 or over to apply for a maintenance assessment on her or his own behalf even where the parents have declined to seek such an assessment.

Education for parenthood

5.12 Local Education Authorities in England and Wales have a duty to provide education for adults to meet local needs. This duty is wide, covering general educational and recreational interests, but it can also cover preparing people for particular events in their lives, such as parenthood. The Scottish Office Education Department's 5-14 Programme guidelines in Personal and Social Development covers this and similar issues for Scotland.

5.13 The Further and Higher Education Act 1992 gives schools powers to provide further education for adults. Schools may well consider putting on courses on parenthood. School governing bodies can decide to put on such courses if there is a demand.

5.14 The National Institute of Adult Continuing Education (NIACE) which is part-funded by the Department for Education, has a role in parent education. NIACE will be publishing a discussion document on guidance on parent education in 1994.

5.15 Schools also teach children about parenthood and family life. Section 1 of the Education Reform Act 1988 requires that the curriculum for all maintained schools should prepare young people for the "opportunities, responsibilities and experiences of adult life". Adult relationships, marriage and parenthood are some of those responsibilities.

5.16 Aspects of family life education are covered in the Science Curriculum. The National Curriculum Council (NCC) recommends that family life education should be a key component of schools' programmes of Personal and Social education. NCC guidance documents on Health Education and Education for Citizenship have been issued to all maintained schools in England. Both cover family life education and ways of integrating it into the curriculum.

5.17 The NHS runs Parentcraft classes for women and their partners as part of their antenatal care.

5.18 Taken together, there is a considerable amount of work going on in the field of parent education. The Government believes the existing statutory framework is adequate to allow for any future development of parent education.

Separation from parents - Article 9

5.19 In England and Wales the Children Act recognises that in general when parents separate or divorce they are the best people to determine questions as to with whom the children should live and with whom they should have contact. If parents are unable to agree the arrangements for the children, a court is able to make a residence order which determines where the child lives and a contact order which decides whom the child is to visit or otherwise have contact with. Both parents retain parental responsibility and are able to make decisions about the child. The concepts of access and custody are abolished by the Act.

5.20 If parents are in disagreement about other aspects of their children's lives it will be open to them to seek a prohibited steps order or a specific issue order to deal with the areas of disagreement.

5.21 When considering whether to make any order the court's first consideration will be the child's welfare. The court will make an order only if to do so is better for the child rather than making no order.

5.22 The Children Act 1989 recognises that children are usually best brought up within their families and requires local authorities to provide family support services to children in need and their families to promote this. The Act promotes increased participation by parents, the child, and others with legitimate interests in the child's welfare, with the aim of reducing the need for court proceedings in cases involving children. The decision to remove a child from home is a last resort after all efforts to support the family in staying together have been exhausted, whilst at the same time the over-riding principle remains that the welfare of the child is paramount.

5.23 The Government proposes in the light of recommendations of the Scottish Law Commission to provide for residence, contact and specific issue orders in Scotland.

Care and Supervision

5.24 In England and Wales compulsory intervention in the care and upbringing of a child is possible only under a court order (although see the section on Article 19 and Police powers to detain a child in a place of safety without a court order). The child, his parents and other people concerned with the child are able to participate in the proceedings. Parents are eligible for legal aid without having to satisfy a merits or means test. The child's interests will be safeguarded by the appointment of a guardian ad litem who will appoint a solicitor to act for the child (unless one has been appointed already by the court).

5.25 The only grounds on which a care or supervision order may be made is that the child is suffering or is likely to suffer significant harm. In an emergency, an application can be made to court for an emergency protection order either to remove the child to accommodation provided by the applicant or to require the child to remain where he is being accommodated at the time of the application. The court can only make the order if it believes that otherwise the child is likely to suffer significant harm. The court can make the order only if they are satisfied that to make the order would be better for the child than to make no order. An application can be heard ex-parte. If this happens, however, parents have the right to challenge it after 72 hours.

5.26   A report on the first full year of the Children Act showed a substantial fall in both the number of children entering compulsory care, and the number of emergency orders made giving authority for the removal of a child from home. The reduction in these orders suggested that local authorities were working in partnership with parents, and were using the power of emergency intervention more appropriately.

5.27   In Scotland compulsory measures of care may be determined by a children's hearing, whether the child has committed an offence or is in need of care and protection. Cases are referred to the court for proof of grounds and also if an appeal is made against the decision of the children's hearing. Conditions of residence and access may be attached to supervision requirements. As outlined in the White Paper "Scotland's Children" the Government propose to amend the law for emergency protection of children where there is good cause to believe that the child is likely to suffer significant harm and removal to a place of safety is necessary for his or her security. The authority for removal will be a new Child Protection Order, granted on the authority of a sheriff.

5.28   Under the Children Act there is a presumption in favour of contact. Children have, subject to certain conditions, the right to apply for contact orders in their own right. The Children Act emphasises the importance of contact between a child looked after by a local authority and parents, relatives, friends etc. The Children Act requires the local authority to allow the child reasonable contact with parents, other persons with parental responsibility, relatives, friends and others connected with him unless it is not reasonably practicable or consistent with the child's welfare. If the local authority wishes to prevent contact between the child and his parents for more than 7 days they must seek a court order to enable them to do so. Parents have the right to challenge this.

Northern Ireland

5.29   In Northern Ireland, the concept of parental authority and the responsibilities attached to being a parent, are very much linked to the concept of custody. As yet, "parental responsibility" is not an established concept in family law and reference is usually made to "parental rights and duties", which comprise the rights to determine a child's education, religion, upbringing and matters relating to a child's property.

5.30   The common law provides that a father is recognised as the natural guardian of his children. The Guardianship of Infants Act 1886 conferred limited rights on a mother to apply to the courts for custody and access, and provided that she should automatically become the child's guardian on the death of the father. A father and mother do not, however, have equal and common responsibility for a child and statute does not equate the mother's position to the natural guardianship of the father, and where, in domestic proceedings a mother is granted legal custody, a father will retain his common law rights in relation to the child. In practice, within the context of the family, parents will exercise the same rights and authority in relation to the child, although where a family breaks down and custody of the child is given to the mother, she will make the majority of the decisions relating to the day to day care of the child.

5.31   Although the concept of "parental responsibility" has not yet been introduced in Northern Ireland, there has been a shift in emphasis in this aspect of family law towards regarding parenthood as a matter of responsibility rather than rights.

5.32   The proposed Children (Northern Ireland) Order rests on the belief that children are generally best looked after within the family with both parents playing a full part in their upbringing without resort to legal proceedings. In support of that tenet, Health and Social Services Boards will have a duty to:-

    i   provide support for children and their families;

    ii   return the child looked after by them to his family unless this is against the child's interests; and

    iii   promote contact between a child and his parents where a child is being looked after by a Board.

5.33   The absence of a judicial review process under current emergency child protection procedures will cease with the implementation of the Children (Northern Ireland) Order, whose provision on this subject will be broadly similar to those of the Children Act 1989.

5.34   Where custody of a child is awarded by a court to one parent, decisions must also be made as to the rights of the non-custodial parent to see the child (access). The legislative provisions governing the particular type of dispute determine the possible orders:

    i.   under the Domestic Proceedings (Northern Ireland) Order 1980 such access may be granted as the court thinks fit.

ii.   Under the Matrimonial Causes (Northern Ireland) Order 1978 such access may be granted as the court thinks fit to such person as the court thinks fit.

5.35 Where the parties are in agreement, the order is usually expressed to be for reasonable access, which leaves precise arrangements regarding the length, frequency and location of the visits to the parties' own discretion. If, however, the parties cannot agree, the court has power to stipulate precisely where and when access is to take place. In certain cases, where the court feels it is necessary, access may be ordered to be supervised.

5.36 In every proceeding involving disputes about access, courts must apply the fundamental principle that the welfare of the child is the first and paramount consideration.

5.37 Under the Children (Northern Ireland) Order a court will be able to make a "contact order", requiring the person with whom the child lives or is to live to allow the child to visit or otherwise have contact with another person.

5.38 In training schools in Northern Ireland policy is that children have the right to maintain contact with their parents, except if it is contrary to the child's best interests.

Social Security Provisions

5.39 The Social Security system's Social Fund provides that a Community Care Grant may be payable to a parent to visit their child who is living with the other parent pending a court hearing to determine the residential responsibility arrangements for the child. This help would enable the estranged parent to remain in contact with their child. The Social Fund may be able to help by providing a Community Care Grant to parents to purchase items to enable children to rejoin the family after being in residential or institutional care. Child Benefit continues to be paid for 12 weeks when a child is in hospital, and indefinitely thereafter provided the family is spending money on the child, for example by paying fares to visit the child in hospital.

Parents who are in prison

5.40 Where a parent is in prison, visits and family contact are very important for the child, who may not fully understand what has happened. Visits from their children help prisoners to remember that they too have a role in parenting and in sharing responsibility for their families in general. For these reasons the prison service is developing many schemes to make the visiting process less alarming for children. More governors are allowing longer visits which give children the opportunity to play with and talk to their imprisoned parents. In permitting this type of visit, which is allowed in addition to the legal minimum visits entitlement, account will be taken of the extent to which the prisoner's behaviour merits it. Many establishments have responded positively to the initiative to provide volunteer supervised play areas in visits rooms; an increasing number of creches have been set up and Visitor's Centres, which offer a shelter where visitors may wait and relax before a visit are now established in most prisons.

5.41 The University of Cambridge Centre for Family Research is currently undertaking a study on Family Ties. At the request of the Prison Service a main topic for study is "Children and Carer" highlighting amongst other concerns the behaviour/problems/changes of children coping with separation from a parent in prison.

Detention following arrest

5.42 A person arrested and detained by the police enjoys the right not to be held incommunicado. He or she may request that one person is informed as soon as possible, and at public expense, of his or her whereabouts. If that person cannot be contacted the person who has made the request may choose up to two alternatives. If they too cannot be contacted the person in charge of detention or of the investigation has discretion to allow further attempts until the information has been conveyed. It is a matter for the detained person to determine whether he or she contacts a family member, or any other person with an interest in his or her welfare. In the case of a juvenile, the custody officer has a specific duty to inform a parent (or, if a parent is not available, another adult with responsibility for a child's welfare) as soon as practicable of the circumstances of the arrest, and ask him or her to come to the police station. This right is additional to the juvenile's right not to be held incommunicado.

Secure Accommodation and Community Homes

5.43 Regulations made under powers in the Children Act 1989 require local authorities to notify parents, or other people with parental responsibility, of an intention to apply to the Court to keep a child in secure accommodation in a Community Home. These current regulatory powers of notification only directly extend to placements in secure accommodation in community homes. They do not apply to secure placements in the health and educational sectors. However, there is a parallel requirement in Magistrates Court Rules to notify parents etc of any application made to the Court concerning the restriction of liberty of a child.

Mothers and Babies in prison

5.44 Where a mother of a young baby comes into conflict with the law, and because of the offence the courts have decided there is no alternative to a custodial sentence, the UK Government is concerned that wherever possible, mothers should have the opportunity where they choose, to keep their babies with them during the crucial early months when bonding is so important. Three of the twelve women's prisons in England and Wales have facilities for mothers and babies providing a total of 38 places. Ten more places will become available soon.

5.45   The decision whether or not to allow mother to keep her baby with her in prison is taken by the Governor, advised by a multidisciplinary team including social services, a paediatrician, health visitor, doctor, probation and prison staff. Provided basic criteria are fulfilled, decisions are taken in the best interests of the child. The age limit for babies in prison is between 9 and 18 months. After 18 months the prison environment is deemed by the Department of Health to be likely to have an adverse effect on the baby's development. The need for babies to be raised in a good child care environment is reflected in the organisation and regime of mother and baby units.

5.46   The Department of Health's Social Services Inspectorate has, at the request of the Home Secretary, undertaken to conduct a series of multi-disciplinary inspections into the 3 Mother and Baby Units which are part of the prison service. The first inspection in 1990 found that routines were not child centred and were not conducive to the development of good parenting skills. Action taken since then has resulted in significant improvements, and the second inspection conducted in 1992 has reported that the Units are offering a service which helps the mothers enjoy their babies and become more skilled as parents. The series of inspections is to continue and its effectiveness will be reviewed.

Immigration decisions involving separation

5.47   The general policy in relation to the removal of parents whose child is in the United Kingdom is guided by our obligations under Article 8 of the European Convention on Human Rights (ECHR) (which protects the right to respect for family life). We are mindful of the fact that, in certain circumstances, the European Court is likely to find a breach of Article 8 where the effect of an immigration decision is to separate a parent from his/her child. Therefore, if an immigration offender has a genuine and subsisting marriage or common-law relationship to someone settled here and there is a child of that marriage/relationship who has the right of abode in the United Kingdom, the presumption is that enforcement action against the parent will not be initiated. This also applies in cases involving divorced or separated parents. Where one parent is settled in the United Kingdom and the removal of the other would result in the deprivation of frequent and regular access currently enjoyed by either parent, enforcement action would not normally be initiated.

Deportation

5.48   It is our general policy to ensure that a family unit is not separated on removal. Although there is the power under Section 3(5)(c) of the

Immigration Act 1971 to deport the families of deportees, in fact this power is rarely used. Our general presumption is that the family of deportees, including all children, will accompany them on removal and the expenses can be met out of public funds. Everything possible is done to encourage the parents to take the child with them on removal, but we do not accept that a foreign national should not be removed simply because they threaten to abandon their child(ren) in this country. Similarly, we see no difficulty in proceeding with the removal of a foreign national parent in cases where a child is made a Ward of Court because of parental abuse or if the foreign national parent is denied contact with a child by a court.

5.49 Although children under the age of 16 who are alone in the United Kingdom without leave can be deported, this is rarely, if ever, carried out. It would only be done where we are satisfied that the child will be met on arrival in his/her home country and that care arrangements were in place thereafter.

Detention under immigration legislation

5.50 Under the Immigration Act 1971 there is the power to detain an immigration offender, either at the port of entry on their arrival in the United Kingdom, or if they overstay their leave, breach conditions attached to it or it is subsequently discovered that they gained entry by practising deception. However, it is not our general policy to detain such an offender under these powers if they are solely responsible for a child in their care and there is no other responsible adult who can care for the child. In cases like this, such persons are given temporary release to enable the parent to remain with the child(ren).

Family reunification - Article 10

5.51 The UK makes generous provision for the admission of foreign children to join parents here. In the period 1980-91 inclusive, some 135,000 children were accepted for settlement. (103,000 in the ten year period 1982-91.)

5.52 There is of course no restriction on the movement of children and family members out of the United Kingdom, save where a court here has directed that a child should not travel abroad, for instance, where custody of a child has been vested in one parent to the exclusion of the other.

5.53 The UK does not accept that there is any absolute right for children to join parents settled here, for example, if they cannot be adequately maintained or accommodated without recourse to public funds, or that parents who have no right to be here should automatically be allowed admission simply because their children are here. All such applications are considered as speedily as possible, with the importance attached to family reunification fully recognised. The report of the working group which drafted the Convention included a formal statement by the Chairman that Article 10 was not intended to affect the general right of States to establish and regulate their respective immigration laws in accordance with their international obligations. (the Chairman also stated that Article 9, which is referred to in Article 10, was intended to apply to domestic, and not international situations). Thus the Convention is not intended to establish any new rights in relation to immigration.

Recovery of maintenance for the child - Article 27, para 4

5.54 The Child Support Agency's objective is to ensure that both parents meet their financial responsibility for their children when they can afford to do so. Regular and adequate payments of maintenance which cover day to day expenditure allow the parent with care to provide for the long-term well-being of the child. Irregular or one-off payments do not allow the parent with care to make such informed choices. In meeting its objective the Child Support Agency aims to provide an effective and professional service to parents and other persons with the care of children to ensure that the appropriate level of maintenance is paid.

5.55 The payment of maintenance is one crucial way in which parents can fulfil their legal and moral obligation to care for their children. The Child Support Agency will remove the responsibility for the assessment, collection and enforcement of child maintenance from the courts in the great majority of cases. The Agency is taking on its duties over a four year period according to a timetable based on the applicants financial circumstances and any existing arrangements.

5.56 In certain circumstances the courts retain jurisdiction to make child maintenance orders, for example where either the child, the person with the care of the child, or the absent parent is not habitually resident in the United Kingdom: where the child is a stepchild of the absent parent; where the child is over the age of 16 and not receiving full-time education; and where a lump sum of property adjustment order is required.

5.57 In addition, courts can still make orders for payment to meet expenses arising from a child's disability, expenses incurred by a child in being educated or training for work; and for additional payments above the Agency's maximum assessment where the absent parent is well off.

5.58 The only family matters affected by the Child Support Act are those connected with maintenance for children. Courts will continue to have their current responsibilities for other related family matters such as assessing spousal maintenance; contact and residence of children; adoption; domestic violence; and disputed paternity.

5.59 The powers of the courts to make financial provision orders in respect of children under the Domestic Proceedings (Northern Ireland) Order 1980 and the Matrimonial Causes (Northern Ireland) Order 1978 are restricted to cases where the child support officer does not have jurisdiction or where the court has jurisdiction to order the absent parent to make payments under a maintenance order in addition to child support maintenance. The court's powers to order financial provision will also be invoked where the absent parent lives outside the jurisdiction.

5.60 The proposed Children (Northern Ireland) Order will set out provisions under which financial relief may be ordered for the benefit of children in proceedings under the Order, which will be without prejudice to the courts' powers to grant relief in matrimonial proceedings in respect of adults as well as children, under the powers conferred by the Matrimonial Causes (Northern Ireland) Order 1978 or the Domestic Proceedings (Northern Ireland) Order 1980, if the issue of financial provision for children arises in the context of matrimonial proceedings. These provisions will be subject to the Child Support (NI) Order 1991 so that where a maintenance assessment is made under that Order, a maintenance order will cease to have effect. Courts will retain their powers to make financial provision orders in respect of children in cases where the child support officer does not have jurisdiction.

Children deprived of a family environment - Article 20

Children in the public care

5.61 Under the Children Act in England and Wales, and child care legislation in Scotland, when a child can no longer remain at home a local authority has to arrange a placement appropriate to his needs. They should first seek to place him in the wider family. If this is not possible he should be placed near to home and kept together with any siblings. In all the decision - making the child's best interests is the guiding principle.

5.62 The placement has to be designed to promote his best interests. The wishes of the child and the parents in the matter should be taken into account. Regard should be had to the child's religious persuasion, racial origin and cultural and linguistic background. The placement might be with foster parents, in a children's home or a residential school depending on what is best for the individual child. In recent years placement with foster parents has been the favoured option particularly in the case of young children.

5.63 The Children Act places particular importance on local authorities planning carefully the care of children being looked after. There was previously evidence of children "drifting" in care. The detailed regulations under the Act on the planning and regular review of children's cases are aimed at bringing about substantial improvements in the care provided for children in whatever setting they are looked after. Improved planning should also help to ensure that children receive greater continuity of care. A lack of continuity is acknowledged to have been a major failing in the past in the arrangements made for certain children in the public care.

5.64 Under the Children Act new regulations were made which are designed to promote the welfare of children who are accommodated away from their parents. The Arrangements for Placement of Children Regulations and the Review of Children's Cases regulations are concerned with ensuring that effective and appropriate planning is undertaken for children and that the arrangements made for their care are monitored regularly to ensure their best interests are being served.

5.65 Children who are fostered are protected by the provisions of the Foster Placement (Children) Regulations. Foster parents have to be approved by the local authority and placements are subject to supervision by the authority to ensure that the child's welfare is being promoted. Foster parents have to enter into written agreements with local authorities about how the child is to be cared for.

5.66 Anybody proposing to foster a child privately has to notify the local authority of their intention to do so and also to advise them when the arrangement ceases. The local authority is placed under a duty to visit the child from time to time in order to promote and safeguard his welfare.

5.67 Before children may be placed for adoption rigorous legal procedures have to be followed. They are discussed in greater detail later in this chapter.

Children's Homes

5.68 Before implementation of the Children Act private children's homes were not subject to regulation. Private homes, local authority homes and voluntary homes are now all subject to the same set of regulations. These are much more detailed than those they replaced. Legislation requires registration and twice-yearly inspection by social services departments of private children's homes to ensure that the required standards are being maintained.

5.69 Voluntary children's homes are required by law to register with the Department of Health or Welsh Office and are to be inspected twice yearly by the Social Services Inspectorate of the Department (by administrative agreement). Social Services Inspectorate, Wales, has its own programme of inspection which includes voluntary children's homes, local authority secure accommodation and services for children with disabilities. Guidance has been issued which requires the twice yearly inspection of local authority children's homes and assisted community homes by local authorities' independent inspection units. The law allows the inspection of any children's home by the Social Services Inspectorate. Regulations require staffing of children's homes to be adequate, in terms of numbers, qualifications and experience, to safeguard and promote the welfare of children accommodated in homes at all times. Guidance advises that all staff should receive individual supervision from their line manager.

Northern Ireland

5.70 When it is necessary for a child to be taken into care in Northern Ireland, the aim is to enable him/her as far as possible to experience family life and under the Department of Health and Social Services' current Regional Strategy, by 1997 at least 75% of children in care, excluding those home-on-trial, must be in a family placement.

5.71 At 30 September 1993 there were 2,155 children in care in Northern Ireland. Of these, 15% were in residential care and 77% in foster care, excluding those home on trial.

5.72 Like the Children Act 1989, one of the key elements of the Children (Northern Ireland) Order will be that Health and Social Services Boards are to have regard to a child's religious persuasion, racial origin and cultural and linguistic background in the provision of services.

5.73 Children who are deprived of their family environment by way of a court disposal in Northern Ireland are sent to Training Schools or the Young Offenders Centre. The Children and Young Persons Act (Northern Ireland) 1968 provides that in such circumstances regard must be paid to the young person's religious persuasion.

5.74 Under the Adoption (Northern Ireland) Order 1987, a parent's consent to adoption may be given subject to conditions with respect to the religious persuasion in which the child is to brought up.

Children from abroad

5.75 There are no provisions within the Immigration Rules which allow for a child to be brought to the United Kingdom specifically for fostering. The Secretary of State may, however, exceptionally exercise his discretion to allow such a child to come here if it is appropriate in all the circumstances of the case. Factors which will be taken into account include the child's circumstances and those of his parent(s) and family abroad; the prospective foster parent's circumstances, including their suitability and capability to care for the child; the reasons for the proposed fostering; the long term plans for the child's future; and whether there is a realistic likelihood of the child leaving this country at the end of the stated period. Once these enquiries are completed, entry clearance may then be granted, if appropriate.

5.76 In instances where a child has applied for, and been granted entry clearance in a category such as that of a student, it may be that at some stage during his period here, he is fostered. While this may be the case, providing the primary reason for him remaining in this country is as a student, and he continues to meet the appropriate requirements of the Immigration Rules relating to students, his immigration status will remain unchanged.

5.77 Children can find themselves in the United Kingdom without their parents in a number of ways: they may have been brought here by their parents and abandoned, and subsequently taken into the care of the local social services; they may have been brought here by their parents and subsequently left in the care of relatives, or placed in private foster care; or they may have been refused leave to enter, but are remaining here while a decision is made on their future.

5.78 It is unlikely that such children would fall within any of the provisions of the Immigration Rules in order for consideration to be given to the question of them remaining here. However, in instances where children are in the care of a relative(s) here, they could qualify if serious and compelling family or other considerations which would make the child's exclusion undesirable, could be shown, together with suitable arrangements made for the child's care; and that the child will be adequately maintained and accommodated without recourse to public funds in accommodation which the relatives own or occupy themselves. The relatives themselves must also be settled here, or have been admitted for settlement here.

5.79 Our aim will normally be that such a child should return to his own country, and be reunited with his natural parents and family. However, in considering such cases, various factors will be taken into account. These will include the views of the local social services towards the possibility and desirability of the child returning to his natural parents and family abroad, and the suitability and capability of those caring for him; the age of the child; and the child's parent's circumstances overseas, together with those of his family overseas.

Children born in the United Kingdom who are not British Citizens

5.80 Children born on or after 1 January 1983 in the United Kingdom will not automatically be British citizens, unless one of their parents (or, in the case of an illegitimate child, the mother), was either a British citizen or settled in the United Kingdom at the time of the child's birth.

5.81 Children in this situation are subject to the requirements of the

Immigration Rules. However, these are not applied until an application for permission for the child to remain here, or to re-enter this country should the child have previously left, is received. In the interim though, the child is not here unlawfully.

5.82 Permission will normally be given for a child to remain here where he has not previously left the United Kingdom, except where the parent(s) or person(s) entrusted with the care of the child are illegal entrants or their period of leave in the United Kingdom has expired, and they do not qualify for a further period, or they are abroad.

5.83 Should such a child leave the United Kingdom and seek to re-enter, he will normally be re-admitted providing the Immigration Officer at the port of entry can be satisfied that the child was born in the United Kingdom on or after 1 January 1993; he is unmarried; is a dependent of his parents, who themselves are lawfully in the United Kingdom, and have a current period of leave; and he has not been absent for longer than two years.

Educational provision

5.84 The Department for Education's guidance Circular 22/89 advises that where a child with special educational needs in England and Wales is in care both the Local Education Authority (LEA) and Social Services Department must recognise the need to co-operate in the best educational, emotional and social interests of the child. To help to ensure the child's educational development a Social Services Department should consult with the LEA in advance and should inform the LEA about every placement they make and should keep the information up to date.

5.85 Regarding pupils being looked after more generally, the Department for Education, in collaboration with the Department of Health, is to issue guidance in due course, after extensive consultation, on the education of such children.

Adoption - Article 21

5.86 Present law and practice guidance complies fully with all the provisions of Article 21.

The principal legislative measures are,

i   Adoption Act 1976

ii   Adoption Agencies Regulations 1983

iii   Adoption Rules 1984

iv   Magistrates Court Rules 1984

v   Children Act 1989

5.87 Broadly similar provisions apply in Scotland under the Adoption (Scotland) Act 1978 and the Adoption Agencies (Scotland) Regulations 1984.

5.88 The legislation is supported by guidance notes issued at intervals on particular aspects of the legislation and on good practice procedures.

5.89 All local authorities in the United Kingdom have a statutory requirement to provide an adoption service. In addition there are a number of adoption agencies approved by the Secretary of State for Health. Approvals must be re-applied for every three years, and are granted following inspection by departmental officials. A mid-term inspection and submission of annual reports supports the process. Both local authority and voluntary agencies are subject to the above legislation.

5.90 This legislation ensures that an adoption order can only be made by a court. The birth parents' agreement to the adoption is necessary. If this cannot be obtained, either because the parents cannot be traced or because they will not agree to adoption, a 'freeing order' may be applied for by the agency with responsibility for the child. As a "freeing order" releases a child for adoption at a later date, the court must be satisfied that the birth parents views, where they can be obtained, are fully taken into account.

5.91 When a freeing order is applied for the court will appoint a reporting officer in respect of the natural parents. The reporting officer who is independent of the adoption is responsible for ensuring that the parents' consent is given willingly, and that all the circumstances relevant to the consent have been investigated. The reporting officer will provide a confidential written report to the court on the completion of his or her investigations.

5.92 Once a child is 'free for adoption' there is no requirement to obtain parental agreement at the subsequent adoption hearing. Legislation governing freeing orders is therefore as exacting as that for adoption orders.

5.93 In order for a court to consider an adoption application an extensive report, called a Schedule 2 report (from Schedule 2 of the Magistrates Court Rules 1984), must be completed. The report contains detailed information, covering physical description, religious background, medical, family and social history on the child, his natural parents, the prospective adoptive parents and the role and involvement of the agency involved. A court may also appoint a Guardian ad litem to represent the child's interest. The child's views on the proposed adoption, if he is old enough to express them are also taken into account.

5.94 The United Kingdom was a party to the recent Hague Conference on Intercountry Adoption and signed the Convention on 12 January 1994. We expect to ratify the Convention in due course.

5.95 On 3 November 1993 the Government published a White Paper on Adoption Law in England and Wales which reflects our view that the best interests of the child are paramount and that the child's view should be sought and reflected in any decisions taken, in so far as a child is able to understand the discussions. A child age 12 or over will have consent to his adoption. A separate document outlining proposed changes to Scottish adoption law will be published in 1994.

5.96 Law and practice in Northern Ireland with regard to adoption does not differ substantively from that in the rest of the United Kingdom. Under the Adoption (Northern Ireland) Order 1987, a parent's consent to adoption may be given subject to conditions with respect to the religious persuasion in which the child is to be brought up.

Inter-country adoption and Immigration

5.97 The Immigration and Nationality Department of the Home Office considers and, where appropriate, authorises permission for a child to travel and be admitted to this country, either as the legally adopted child of his parents, or effectively for adoption through the Courts here.

5.98 The Immigration Rules make provision for children to be admitted to the United Kingdom for settlement with their adoptive parent or parents from both overseas countries whose adoption orders are recognised for the purposes of United Kingdom law, ('designated' countries), and any country where it is satisfactorily demonstrated that a 'de-facto' adoption has taken place. Although not provided for by the Immigration Rules, children may also, exceptionally, be admitted to the United Kingdom for the purpose of adoption here by their prospective adoptive parents, either where no overseas adoption has taken place, or the child has been adopted in a country whose adoption orders are not recognised as valid for the purposes of United Kingdom law, ('non-designated' countries).

5.99 In the case of children adopted in a 'designated' country, or where a 'de-facto' adoption has taken place, prior entry clearance must be obtained from the nearest British Diplomatic Post to their overseas address which is designated to issue settlement entry clearances, before they travel here. In order to qualify for admission, the entry clearance officer will need to be satisfied that the adoption involved a genuine transfer of parental responsibility on the grounds of the original parents' inability to care; that the adoption is not one of convenience arranged to facilitate the child's admission here; that the adoptive parents are settled here, or are being admitted for settlement; and that the child will be adequately maintained and accommodated without recourse to public funds in accommodation which the adoptive parents occupy or will occupy themselves.

5.100 In the case of a claimed 'de-facto' adoption, it will additionally have to be shown that the adoptive parents have for a substantial period of time, been treating the child as their own natural child and accepted all the responsibilities which that involves, to the exclusion of the child's natural parents and any family they may have. Should these requirements be satisfied, entry clearance will usually be granted. (The recognition and acceptance of the existence of a de-facto adoption is one purely for the purposes of immigration and nationality, and confers no legal status on the relationship under United Kingdom law. The adoptive parents are advised to seek to re-adopt the child through the Courts here.)

5.101 Upon arrival in the United Kingdom, the child will normally be admitted for settlement if his adoptive parents are settled here. However, if one or both of the adoptive parents has a limited period of leave in this country, the period of leave granted to the child will normally be in line with that of the parent with the lesser period of leave.

5.102 In cases involving a child who has not been adopted overseas, or who has been adopted in a 'non-designated' country, an application for entry clearance will normally be considered on the basis that the child would be travelling to the United Kingdom for the purpose of adoption here. Although there are no provisions within the Immigration Rules for a child to travel to the United Kingdom for this purpose, the Secretary of State may, exceptionally, exercise his discretion to allow such a child to come here if it is appropriate in all the circumstances of the case. Permission for a child to travel to the United Kingdom for this purpose must be applied for, and obtained from the nearest British Diplomatic Post to the child's overseas address designated to issue settlement entry clearances before he travels here.

5.103 Once an application for entry clearance has been made, the entry clearance officer will consider both the child's circumstances, and those of his family overseas, and then normally refer the application the Immigration Department in the United Kingdom for a decision.

5.104 As with a 'designated' country and 'de-facto' adoption case, it will have to be satisfactorily demonstrated that the adoption (will) involve(d) a genuine transfer of parental responsibility on the grounds of the original parents' inability to care; that the adoption is not one of convenience arranged to facilitate the child's admission here; that the prospective adoptive parents are settled here, or are being admitted for settlement; and that the child will be adequately maintained and accommodated without recourse to public funds in accommodation which the prospective adoptive parents own or occupy themselves. If these requirements are met, additional advice will be sought from the appropriate territorial Health Department on whether it would be in the child's best interests to travel here for adoption by the prospective adoptive parents. To this end the local authority social services department will normally be asked to carry out a home study report on the prospective adoptive parents to assess their suitability, and consider whether the proposed adoption would safeguard and promote the interests of the child throughout his childhood. Once these enquiries have been satisfactorily completed, entry clearance may then be granted.

5.105   Upon arrival, the child will normally be admitted for a period of 12 months to enable the adoption process to be instigated here. Upon application to the Immigration and Nationality Department, further periods of leave to remain will usually be granted to enable the Court to consider an adoption application. Should a Court in the United Kingdom grant an adoption order, the child will automatically acquire British citizenship by virtue of Section 1(5) of the British Nationality Act, 1981, providing (at least one of) the adopting parent(s) are British Citizens on the date the adoption order is made. If this is the case, the child will be free of immigration control, and able to travel to and from the United Kingdom as frequently as he wishes; and to remain here for an indefinite period. If the child does not automatically acquire British citizenship, his citizenship will remain unchanged, although he will, upon application, usually be granted leave to remain in line with the adoptive parent who has the lesser period of leave.

Illicit transfer and non-return - Article 11

5.106   The criminal law on the abduction of children in England and Wales is to be found in the Child Abduction Act 1984.

5.107   Under section 1 of the Act, it is an offence for a person connected with a child under 16 to take or send that child out of the United Kingdom without the appropriate consent. A person is connected with the child if he or she is its parent, guardian, or has legal custody, and an offence may be committed if he or she sends or takes that child abroad without the consent of the other parent, guardian, custodian of the child, or, if, the child is the object of a custody order, the consent of the court. The section 1 offence is aimed chiefly at so-called "tug-of-love" cases, where one parent tries to take the child abroad without the other's knowledge or consent, as might occur, for example, following a divorce where there was dispute over the custody of the child. Section 6 of the Act makes it an offence in Scotland for a person connected with a child to take or send the child outside the UK in defiance of an order by a court anywhere in the UK.

5.108   Under section 2 of the Act it is an offence for any person, not 'connected' with the child to take or detain a child under 16 without lawful authority or reasonable excuse. This cannot be committed by a parent, guardian or someone with legal custody of the child. There is no Scottish equivalent of Section 2 applying to persons not connected with the child since the matter is covered by common law.

5.109   The UK has implemented the Hague Convention on the Civil Aspects of International Child Abduction and the European Convention on Recognition and Enforcement of Decisions Concerning Custody of Children and on Restoration of Custody of Children, both of which protect children by requiring contracting states to recognise and enforce custody orders and to return children wrongly removed or retained away from their country of habitual residence. Under the conventions each country has a central authority which deals with requests from other convention countries for the return of children who have been wrongfully removed from their homes. The central theme of the conventions is that decisions relating to a child's custody and access should be decided in their home country. The UK has a well-recognised international reputation for carrying out its obligations under the Conventions. The courts in England and Wales will also apply the principles of the Hague Convention to cases of child abduction involving states which are not parties to the Convention.

5.110   The United Kingdom is party to the 1921 International Convention for the Suppression of the Traffic in Women and Children and the 1956 Supplementary Convention on the Abolition of Slavery.

5.111   The UK plays an active part in international human rights fora on the issue of child exploitation, including the illicit transfer of children abroad. During the 48th Commission on Human Rights (CHR), we co-sponsored a resolution implementing a Programme of Action for the prevention of the sale of children, child prostitution and child pornography. We also supported the renewal of the mandate of the Special Rapporteur on the Sale of Children. CHR49 resolution 1993/79 on the elimination of child labour, which received UK support, specifically underlined the duties of states to apply principle 9 of the Declaration on the Rights of the Child: "The child shall be protected against all forms of neglect, cruelty and exploitation. He shall not be the subject of traffic in any form." As holder of the EC Presidency during the 47th UN General Assembly, the UK introduced a resolution on street children, an initiative which has been further developed at subsequent sessions of the Commission and the UN General Assembly.

5.112   The Child Abduction Unit within the Lord Chancellor's Department is a central authority for England and Wales. It offers considerable practical assistance when children have been removed and taken to or from a convention country. The unit handles the requests for the return of these children. It is organised to deal with cases quickly and efficiently including offering practical advice at a very difficult time for those involved. Support for children's rights in this area is also provided by the Parliamentary Working Party on Child Abduction, which recently produced a report called "Home and Away", making a number of recommendations, and the voluntary organisation "Reunite", the National Council for Abducted

Children.

5.113   The following table shows the number of people proceeded against and found guilty of child abduction under the Child Abduction Act 1984 in England and Wales from 1987 to 1991:

	1987	1988	1989	1990	1991
Total prosecuted	52	56	67	66	89
Total found guilty	35	26	42	33	45

5.114   There also exists a common law offence of kidnapping, which is applicable to child kidnapping. No prosecution can be instituted for an offence of kidnapping if it was committed against a child under 16, or by a person connected with a child as defined in section 1 of the Child Abduction Act 1984, except by or with the consent of the Director of Public Prosecutions. Figures for prosecutions for kidnapping, where the victim was a child are not centrally collated since the offence is not age specific.

Abuse and neglect - Article 19

5.115   The Children Act 1989 provides a range of court orders to enable the correct balance to be struck between the rights of parents to bring up their children and the duty of the state to intervene when necessary to protect the child.

Child Protection

5.116   The child protection provisions of the Act are designed to promote appropriate and decisive action to protect children from abuse or neglect, combined with reasonable opportunities for parents, the children themselves and others to present their points of view. Government guidance has stressed the need to involve parents and children where they are of sufficient age and understanding in all meetings where decisions will be made which will affect the child's welfare or future upbringing. As a normal rule, parents would be invited to all child protection conferences except where their presence or likely disruptive behaviour would prevent proper consideration of the welfare of the child. The conference is expected to have a clear up to date account of the child's views where the child is too young or does not wish to attend the conference. If parents are not invited to conferences the guidance requires that the reasons should be clearly stated and conveyed to the parents.

5.117   Under the Children Act statutory responsibility for the care and protection of children who may be at risk of abuse rests with the local authority social services departments, with health services, probation, police, education and voluntary organisations also involved wherever appropriate. Local authorities have a statutory duty to investigate information received suggesting that a child may need protection. The Government has provided guidance on inter-agency co-operation for the protection of children from abuse for all involved agencies, and all areas have agreed procedures to facilitate inter-agency communication and co-operation.

5.118   Central to this inter-agency co-operation is the Area Child Protection Committee, the recognised joint forum for developing and monitoring child protection policies. At a national level the Inter-Departmental Group on Child Abuse, comprising senior officials from a number of Government Departments, meets regularly to discuss cross-sector issues in relation to child protection.

5.119   Locally, each Social Services Department holds a central register which lists all the children in the area who are considered to be at risk of abuse and therefore who are currently the subject of an inter-agency plan to protect them. Registration takes place as a result of a child protection conference which will decide whether a child is at risk of abuse and whether the child's name should be placed on the Register. If a child's name is placed on the Register the conference will also draw up an inter-agency agreement to work co-operatively to protect the child.

5.120   The Government has given grants totalling over £3 million for a centrally-funded initiative to produce child protection training materials for generalists, specialists and managers from different professional disciplines, and awareness materials for the wider public. It also funded a survey to establish the nature and range of treatment facilities for abused children and young perpetrators, which has informed the deployment of resources on a centrally-funded treatment initiative since 1990. In addition, as part of the Department of Health's overall child care research programme, there is an extensive range of research projects in relation to child abuse.

5.121   The Department of Health and Welsh Office have also provided practice guidance to social workers involved in assessment of child abuse cases, professional guidance on diagnosis of child sexual abuse, issued to all doctors in the country, and professional guidance for senior nurses on the management of child abuse work.

Police powers in cases of abuse

5.122   The police have extensive powers to protect children from abuse, regardless of the nature of the child's relationship to the alleged abuser. Under the Children Act the police have an emergency power to detain a child in a place of protection for a limited period without prior application to the court. They can obtain a warrant under the Children Act to enter premises and search for children. In emergencies, where there is no time to apply for a warrant, the police may enter premises in order to save life and limb under the Police and Criminal Evidence Act.

Role of the education service in child protection

5.123   The Department for Education issued guidance to all Local Education Authorities (LEAs) and maintained schools in England and Wales in Circular 4/88,"Working Together for the Protection of Children from Abuse: Procedures within the Education Service." This guidance makes clear that the primary responsibility for the protection of children from abuse rests with local authority social services departments (SSDs). The NSPCC and the police also have statutory responsibilities, and they along with SSDs are the principal agencies involved in investigating and dealing with individual cases. Although education staff should not investigate allegations or suspicions of abuse but should refer cases to the local SSD, the guidance recognises that teachers are in good position to identify possible signs, or hear allegations of, abuse. Each school should therefore have a teacher with designated responsibility for coordinating action within the school and for liaison with other agencies. Each LEA should have a designated official for coordinating policy and action, especially promulgating procedures to be followed by its schools. Those procedures should include guidance on dealing with cases where a member of a school's staff is accused of abuse.

5.124   The guidance in Circular 4/88 to maintained schools was briefly reiterated in a section on the education service in the interagency guidance, "Working Together under the Children Act 1989", which appeared in October 1991. That guidance also, however, covered independent schools. For those schools, there is the same need for staff to refer cases of possible abuse to SSDs but the onus is put on SSDs to ensure that such schools are aware of the local interagency procedures. Their proprietors should make sure that appropriate procedures, including procedures for dealing with allegations against members of staff, are in place in their schools.

Bullying in schools

5.125   The Government believes that all schools should act firmly against bullying wherever and whenever it appears. To help them do so, the Department for Education distributed practical guidance in the form of the "Action Against Bullying" pack to all schools in England in July 1992. To emphasise the importance attached to the issue, Schools Minister Eric Forth wrote a personal letter to chairmen of governors and other key agencies commending the pack to their attention. A similar pack was distributed in Scotland.

5.126   The Department for Education is also considering how best to provide further guidance to schools on eliminating bullying, drawing on the outcomes of recently completed DFE-funded research at Sheffield University.

Scotland

5.127   The Social Work (Scotland) Act 1968 provides the legal framework for the protection of children from harm. Where a child may need compulsory measures of care to secure his or her welfare cases are referred to children's hearings for decision. Local Authorities are responsible for providing preventative care and compulsory measures at home, with foster carers and in residential settings. The Government has fostered close co-operation between the services in protecting children. Child Protection Committees have been developed as the means of coordinating services in each area. A new system of management information has been introduced to help local authorities to plan and control resources devoted to child protection. New practice methods are being developed to bring the behaviour of abusers under control and so prevent further abuse of children. As a major part of improving staff skills an extensive training programme has been maintained with strong financial backing from the Government. Finally, new guidance is being prepared on

    i   Cooperation between agencies

    ii   Social work practice in dealing with sexual abuse

    iii   Joint investigation and interviewing by social workers and police

Northern Ireland

5.128   Increasing numbers of reported and suspected cases of child abuse have been arising each year in Northern Ireland.

5.129   The Northern Ireland strategy for dealing with the problem is part of a wider national strategy based on improved training, development of appropriate procedures and legislation.

5.130   Funding for additional training for staff involved in tackling child abuse has been provided.

5.131   Guidance on procedures for prevention, detection and management of child abuse has been issued to promote the development and strengthening of local procedures and funding to help implement the guidance has been provided. Area Child Protection Committees have been established to plan and co-ordinate local procedures for the protection of children.

5.132   Additional funds have been provided to reduce the incidence of child abuse through positive action aimed at supporting families and raising awareness amongst children, and developing assessment and treatment programmes for abused children and child and adolescent abusers. Work has started with juvenile abusers, with 3 centres operating on a multidisciplinary basis and offering structured group programmes. Two of these centres are included in a national evaluation of the effectiveness of treatment programmes.

5.133   Strategic targets for child protection, covering prevention, protection and treatment for both abused children and abusers, are set in the Regional Strategy for the Northern Ireland Health and Personal Social Services for 1992-97.

5.134   Article 19 has implications for procedures in Training Schools. A criminal justice review is currently underway in Northern Ireland which will include consideration of the issues involved and how to address them.

Physical chastisement of children

5.135   The Government's policy on the physical punishment of children is that it has no place in the child care environment and this has been implemented in England and Wales through the Children Act Regulations and Guidance. Physical Punishment in State Schools is prohibited, as it is in Independent Schools where the fees of the pupil are paid by a public body. In children's homes the use of corporal punishment, deprivation of food and drink, requirement to wear inappropriate clothing and deprivation of sleep is prohibited.

5.136   As regards corporal punishment of children, while not prohibited in law, in practice the Health and Social Services Boards in Northern Ireland do not permit its use in residential care, foster care or day care settings. Nor is it allowed in voluntary children's homes. The proposed Children (Northern Ireland) Order and subsequent Regulations and Guidance will give this situation the force of law. Corporal punishment in grant-aided schools in Northern Ireland is prohibited by law. Independent schools are very few in number. There is no evidence of the use of corporal punishment in these schools.

5.137   In the UK Government's view Article 19 has to be read in conjunction with Article 5 which obliges States to respect a parent's responsibilities to provide appropriate direction and guidance in the exercise by the child of the rights recognised in the present convention. The UK Government's view is that appropriate direction and guidance includes the administration, by the parent, of reasonable and moderate physical chastisement to a child. The single most important responsibility for ensuring a child grows up to abide by the law rests with the parents. A firm but fair approach to discipline is an important part of this.

Unacceptable physical chastisement

5.138   Excessive punishment amounting to abuse is, of course, a criminal offence, and so it must remain. The Government believes that the law deals fully and firmly with the abuse of children in this country, but it is aware of the need constantly to monitor and review the strength of the law. There are various statutes under which a person may be charged where excessive punishment is used and these together with the maximum penalties available to the courts are as follows:

Common law offence of assault	-	imprisonment of up to 3 months' or a fine not exceeding £5,000 or both
Assault occasioning actual bodily harm, Section 47, Offences Against the Person Act 1861	-	imprisonment of up to 5 years
Grievous Bodily Harm or Wounding, Section 20 of the Offences Against the Person Act 1861	-	imprisonment of up to 5 years
Grievous Bodily Harm or Wounding with Intent, Section 18 of the Offences Against the Person Act 1861	-	imprisonment of up to life
Section 1, Children and Young Persons Act 1933	-	Imprisonment of up to 10 years (following an increase from 2 years in the Criminal Justice Act 1988)

5.139   Parents have a duty of care towards their children and a failure to fulfil that duty may result in a conviction for child cruelty under section 1 of the Children and Young Persons Act 1933 which covers assaults, ill-treatment, abandoning or exposing a child.

5.140   The table below shows the number of people proceeded against and found guilty of offences of child cruelty under section 1 of the Children and Young Persons Act 1933 (the maximum penalty for which is 10 years' imprisonment) in England and Wales from 1987

	1987	1988	1989	1990	1991
Total prosecuted	145	228	375	440	424
Total found guilty	143	164	211	247	234

Periodic review of placement - Article 25

Children in the public care

5.141   The Children Act guidance exhorts local authorities to ensure that the system for reviewing a child's placement provides for the full participation of both children and parents in the decision making process. The involvement of the child is subject to his understanding and welfare, and the possibility of the child being accompanied to the meeting by a person able to provide friendly support should be considered. The Children Act guidance advises, however, that the child's attendance should be the norm. The involvement of child and parents in a review meeting is in line with the basic philosophy of the Children Act in relation to participation, the wishes and feelings of the child and his parents and the spirit of partnership between the local authority and the parents.

5.142   In Scotland local authorities have a duty to review at no more than 6 monthly intervals children who are in their care. Many authorities carry out reviews more frequently. The Government proposes to enhance and raise the standard of reviews by prescribing their form and content in regulations.

5.143   The first reviews of the child's case should take place not later than four weeks after the child begins to be looked after. The second review should take place not more than three months after the first review. Subsequent reviews should take place at intervals of not more than six months. This is a minimum standard. Reviews should be held as often as necessary to promote the child's welfare.

5.144   The Children (Secure Accommodation) Regulations 1991 require local authorities to review periodically the case of a child who is detained in secure accommodation and in any case within one month of the start of the placement. The local authority is required to appoint at least three people to review the case of each child placed in secure accommodation to satisfy itself that the statutory criteria continue to apply. In order to strengthen the arrangements for these reviews, further regulations (Children (Secure Accommodation) Amendment Regulations) were introduced in October 1992. These stipulate that the constitution of the placement review panel should include at least one person who is neither an officer or a member of the local authority. In other words a member who is independent and able to represent the interests of the child. In addition the local authority looking after the child is now required to state publicly what action it takes as a result of the review.

5.145   While there is currently no legal requirement for Health and Social Services Boards in Northern Ireland to review children in care, it has been a policy requirement for some years.

5.146   Provision in the proposed Children (Northern Ireland) Order and Regulations will prescribe the duties on Health and Social Services Boards as to the frequency and manner of reviews of children in their care.

Reviews of cases of children detained under Mental Health legislation

5.147   The vast majority of children in hospitals and units because of mental illness are informal patients who are not detained under The Mental Health Act 1983, the governing legislation in England and Wales concerning the detention in hospital of people suffering from a mental disorder. However, for those who are detained, the legislation applying in the UK concerning their rights is set out in the following paragraphs.

5.148   People of any age can be detained in hospital under the Mental Health Act 1983, if the criteria are met. However, a person must have attained the age of 16 years to be received into guardianship under section 7 of the Act. Detention of a person in hospital, either for assessment or treatment, is properly and entirely a matter for the clinical judgement of the doctors concerned and people may only be detained if the strict criteria laid down in the Mental Health Act 1983 are met. Briefly, these are: firstly, that the patient must be suffering from a mental disorder as defined by the Act; secondly, the mental disorder must be of a nature or degree which makes admission to the hospital appropriate; thirdly, medical treatment must be necessary for the health or safety of the patient, or for the protection of other persons.

5.149   The power to admit a patient under the Act is clear and rightly rests with the professionals concerned, the doctors who must provide medical recommendations and the social worker who makes the application.

5.150   Decisions relating to matters such as voluntary admission may be made on behalf of incompetent minors by parents or those with parental responsibility. However, children who are judged to be competent to admit themselves voluntarily, even those under the age of 16, may give valid consent to this course of action.

5.151   The Mental Health Act Commission was established under the 1983 Act to protect the interests of detained patients. The Commission has a number of responsibilities including the investigation of complaints made by or about detained patients. It also operates and keeps under review the 'consent to treatment' provisions in the Mental Health Act, including the appointment of doctors and others to give second opinions when a patient refuses or is unable to give consent to certain forms of treatment or when the treatment is one that always requires a second opinion before it can be given.

5.152   Children detained under mental health legislation in England and Wales have exactly the same rights as adults and these are explained to them on admission both verbally and in writing (the Department of Health produces information leaflets on all sections under which a patient can be detained). These include review by the Managers or an application to a Mental Health Review Tribunal (MHRT) for consideration of the need for continued detention.

5.153   A patient can ask the hospital managers to review the need for continued detention at any time. The nearest relative can also ask for a patient's discharge but this can be overruled if the doctor makes a report to the Managers, barring a nearest relative's discharge application.

5.154   All detained patients can make an application to an MHRT once during every period of detention. If a patient has not had a Tribunal for 3 years (1 year in the case of a patient under 16 years of age) the hospital Managers must refer his case to a Tribunal. The MHRT is an independent body consisting of individuals who will all have considerable experience in the mental health field. The MHRT has the power to discharge a patient if continued detention in hospital is no longer necessary.

5.155   Under the Mental Health (Scotland) Act 1984 the Mental Welfare Commission for Scotland exercises protective functions in respect of persons who may by reason of disorder, be incapable of adequately protecting themselves or their interests.

5.156   The Commission takes careful note of the use of the Mental Health Act in respect of people under 16 and attempts to examine the circumstances in which it has been judged necessary to section a child under the terms of the Act. The Commission also pays attention to what dictates the use of the Mental Health (Scotland) Act 1984 in some cases and parental consent in others. The Commission has included in its 1994 visiting programme a round of visits to child psychiatry units as a priority. The Commission is an independent body.

5.157   In Northern Ireland the Mental Health (Northern Ireland) Order 1986 is the governing legislation concerning the detention in hospital of people suffering from a mental disorder. While there are some differences between it and the Mental Health Act 1983, the position described above is generally true also in Northern Ireland.

5.158   The following tables refer to England and Wales.

CHILDREN LOOKED AFTER IN RESIDENTIAL ACCOMMODATION AND FOSTER PLACEMENTS AT 31 MARCH 1992 BY AGE GROUP

	AGE						
	<1	1-4	5-9	10-15	16-17	18+	Total
Total of all Children Looked After	1400	7900	11400	21200	11900	550	54400
In Residential Accommodation:							
Community Homes with education facilities	-	10	20	670	290	10	990
Other Community Homes	20	120	620	4000	2100	80	6900
Voluntary Homes	10	20	120	340	330	30	850
Private Registered Homes	*	30	90	260	130	*	510
Schools	*	*	60	570	220	20	860
Foster Placements	1000	5100	7500	12500	5100	190	31300
Other remaining placements	400	2700	3000	2900	3800	200	13000

- indicates zero figures

* = Less than 5 children accommodated

Figures are rounded to the nearest 10 or 100 as appropriate and may not add because of rounding

CHILDREN LOOKED AFTER UNDER POLICE PROTECTION ORDERS/EMERGENCY PROTECTION ORDERS AT 31 MARCH 1992 BY AGE GROUP

	AGE						
	<1	1-4	5-9	10-15	16-17	18+	Total
Number of Children	20	30	20	20	*	*	90

* = Less than 5 children accommodated

Figures are rounded to the nearest 10 and may not add because of rounding

Chapter 6: Basic Health and Welfare

Survival and development - Article 6, para 2

Sudden Infant Death Syndrome

6.1   A major contribution to the achievement of reductions in infant mortality has been made by the "Back to Sleep Campaign" aimed at reducing sudden infant death. Until recently in England and Wales over 1,000 infants a year succumbed to cot deaths.

6.2   During 1991 there was a growing scientific consensus that the sleeping position of an infant was a major risk factor in relation to cot death. An expert group examined the evidence and advised that infants should not be laid to sleep on their fronts (except in particular circumstances upon medical advice); and that the great majority of infants should be nursed on their backs. A publicity campaign was mounted to put across this advice to families with new babies. The rate of Sudden Infant Death Syndrome in England and Wales in the postneonatal period (deaths after the first month of life and before the first year) has been falling since it reached the peak of 2.01 per 1000 live births in 1988. Following the launch of the "Back To Sleep" campaign in December 1991, the rate has fallen substantially (by almost 50%) - from 1.25 per 1000 live births in 1991 to 0.63 per 1000 in 1992.

Immunisation

6.3   Childhood immunisation, and the part it has played in reducing and eliminating a number of terrible diseases which most of us can remember, is another of the most heartening successes in our preventive health programme. The diseases included in the childhood immunisation programme are:

i   diphtheria, tetanus and pertussis (whooping cough) for which a combined vaccine called DTP is available,

ii   measles, mumps and rubella for which a combined vaccine called MMR is available

iii   polio

iv   and, since 1 October 1992, haemophilus influenzae b, or Hib as it is known, which is the main cause of a form of bacterial meningitis in young children.

6.4   The success of the programme has resulted in the incidence of childhood diseases dropping to their lowest ever levels. Indigenous diphtheria and neonatal tetanus no longer occur and measles and whooping cough are now rarities in family doctors' surgeries. No child in England and Wales has died from acute measles-related illness since 1989. Additionally, the World Health Organisation (WHO) have recognised the United Kingdom as one of the countries which have eliminated indigenous polio due to wild virus.

6.5   The WHO target of 90% immunisation coverage adopted by the Government in 1985 has been reached or exceeded for all diseases except for Hib for which figures have yet to be received. The Public Health Laboratory Service's COVER (Cover of Vaccination Evaluated Rapidly) programme shows that, at August 1993, 95% of children aged 18 months had received diphtheria, tetanus and polio immunisations and 93% had received pertussis, whilst 93% of children aged 24 months had received measles, mumps and rubella immunisation. The new target of 95% immunisation uptake by 1995 adopted by the Government and set out in "The Health of the Nation" White Paper is within reach.

6.6   The most recent addition to the vaccine programme, Hib, has shown dramatic and exciting early results since it came in October 1992, with a 70% reduction in reports of invasive haemophilus diseases in the first quarter of 1993, when compared with the same period for the three previous years.

6.7   Doctors and nurses in both general practice and the community health service are to be most warmly congratulated on these excellent achievements.

6.8   These achievements are all the more remarkable because immunisation is not compulsory in the United Kingdom as, with a few exceptions provided for under the law, people in the UK are free to choose whether or not they receive medical treatment or prophylaxis for any particular condition. Government policy remains one of education and advice and the latest statistics confirm the success of this approach.

Disabled children - Article 23

Children in the public care

6.9   It is generally agreed that all children benefit from the opportunity to grow up in a family setting. In the case of children looked after who have a disability it is often more difficult for local authorities to find a suitable foster family placement. Since the early 1980s, however, there has been a significant growth in successful foster placements for children with a range of disabilities. Social services departments have the main responsibility but a number of voluntary agencies also provide specialist fostering services for children with disabilities.

6.10 Children's homes governed by the Children's Homes Regulations which accommodate children with disabilities are required to provide the necessary equipment, facilities and adaptions for children with a disability.

The Children Act and services for disabled children

6.11 The Children Act 1989, which applies in England and Wales, defines all disabled children as being in need. Local authorities' responsibilities towards them are set out in the same way as those for other children in need. Local authorities are required to keep a separate register of children with disabilities in their area, to assist service planning and monitoring. Authorities must also provide services to minimise the effect of disabilities on the children and give them an opportunity to live as normal a life as possible and to ensure that the accommodation they live in is not unsuitable for their needs.

6.12 The Children (Northern Ireland) Order will include similar provision for disabled children.

6.13 Welfare services for children with disabilities in Scotland are provided for under the Social Work (Scotland) Act 1968. The Government have announced their intention to strengthen the law affecting disabled children in Scotland.

6.14 The services offered by authorities for children with disabilities include advice and counselling both to the children and their parents, preparing the children for independence, respite care which may provide a welcome break both for the children and their parents, and full-time accommodation for the children with the most severe problems. Government guidance encourages authorities to provide services within a planned package of care.

Education

6.15 As said in the introduction to this report, where the education of pupils with special educational needs is concerned, the Education Act 1981 in England and Wales, in Scotland the Education (Scotland) Act 1980, already established the essential principles enshrined in paragraphs 2 and 3 of Article 23 of the Convention. The Government believes that the measures in the Education Act 1993, which applies in England and Wales, will further improve the education of children with special needs by:

    i   continuing to facilitate the integration of children with special needs into mainstream schools;

ii   giving increased parental rights to express a preference for particular schools;

iii   prescribing time limits for the assessment of such children; and

iv   streamlining the procedures for appeal against perceived inadequate provision for these children by Local Education Authorities.

6.16 The Government has also promoted, and will continue to promote, improved access for disabled children in mainstream schools.

Social Security

6.17 Research is presently underway to determine the effectiveness of social security benefits available to families with disabled children. It is intended that a report of the findings will be issued next year.

6.18 Also mentioned in the introduction was the help the Government has given to families with disabled children - it is estimated that:

i   the extension of help with care needs for children under 2 will help some 3,000 people at a cost of £6m (introduced in April 1990);

ii   the new rates of Disability Living Allowance, for the less severely disabled, have already helped some 272,000 people including children;

iii   increases in the child's disability premium will help about 20,000 at a cost of £8m (introduced in April 1990);

iv   the introduction of the carer premium, which includes help for caring for disabled children (in April 1990) will help some 30,000 at a cost of £15m.

Children with mobility problems

6.19 The Department of Transport's Mobility Unit continues to encourage and monitor projects to improve access to transport for all people with disabilities. The Department worked closely with the Disabled Persons' Transport Advisory Committee over the production of the recently re-issued "Recommended Specification for Buses Used to Operate Local Services" which includes a wide range of simple low-cost features which greatly improve access to buses for passengers such as parents carrying small children.

6.20 The Department of Transport is also currently supporting two demonstration projects of buses with low flat floors which are fully accessible to everyone, including wheelchair users. The Mobility Unit also works closely with Light Rapid Transit operators and British Rail over access issues. All InterCity trains are now fully wheelchair accessible.

6.21 On the specific issue of children with mobility problems, the Department of Transport has produced a video and supporting literature entitled "It's Not My Problem" which is designed to promote better quality special needs transport services for children and young people who need specialised provision to get to school, attend a youth club, or go on holiday for example.

Equal opportunities

6.22 The UK played an active role in the elaboration of the Standard Rules on the Equalisation of Opportunities for Disabled Persons, which were adopted by the UN General Assembly in December 1993. The UK also participated in the Ministers' Working Group on disability in January 1993 which decided to create an international mechanism for ministers to promote cooperation and international exchange with respect to the status of persons with disabilities. This initiative was welcomed in CHR49 resolution 1993/29 on Human Rights and Disability, which was co-sponsored by the UK.

Overseas Aid under this Article

6.23 The UK Government is concerned to make information provision and exchange a necessary and priority component of projects dealing with disabled children whenever this need arises. An example of this is in Andhra Pradesh, where the Overseas Development Administration is collaborating with the Indian Ministries of Education and Health, where one component of the programme is the training of health workers and teachers to identify hearing and sight disabilities.

Health and health services - Article 24

Health Promotion

6.24 There has been a lengthy and sustained improvement in the health of children in the UK and in the provision of health care and welfare for them. Formal health strategies apply throughout the UK. These have differences within the UK. For example the Government's health promotion strategy for England and Wales "The Health of the Nation" (July 1992) selected 5 target areas : heart disease, cancers, mental illness, sexual health and accidents. The Scottish Health Strategy "Scotland's Health - A Challenge to Us All" (July 1992) however has coronary heart disease, cancers, HIV/AIDS, accidents and dental and oral health as its priorities. To illustrate the application of these strategies to child health, the situation in England is used as an example in this section of the report.

6.25 The promotion of a healthy lifestyle in childhood is critical to the achievement of all the targets. The "Health of the Nation" strategy recognises the need for a safe and healthy home environment in which children may develop to their full potential and commits the Government to the objective of ensuring that decent housing is within the reach of every family. There are a number of schemes, some directly funded by the Department of Health, designed to improve access to health services by homeless people, including families in bed and breakfast accommodation (The use of bed and breakfast accommodation by local authorities for homeless households fell by 41% in the twelve months to September 1993) and we hope that the fact that all health regions are being asked this year to examine the adequacy of primary health care for homeless people will accelerate progress.

Health in Wales

6.26 The series of protocols for Investment in Health Gain produced by the Welsh Health Planning Forum between 1990 and 1993 examine the 10 health gain areas identified in a Strategic Intent, or strategy as having the most impact on the health of the people of Wales. The protocols assess areas for intervention and recommend targets for health gain and service delivery. Issues such as sudden infant death syndrome, childhood immunisation and nutrition are dealt with fully in the Maternal and Early Child Health protocol. The Health Environments protocol covers problems such as drinking water and air pollution, whilst oral health and road safety matters are covered by the Oral Health protocol and Injuries protocol respectively.

6.27 It has been recognised, however, that there are particular areas relating to children which make it appropriate that the protocol should be supplemented by a separate document and 'Health and Social Gain for Children' was issued in August 1993. The Health and Social Gain for Children document aims to draw together the existing guidance comprehensively whilst being selective in its coverage of protocol guidance.

6.28 The document is based on a set of principles, the philosophy of which is embodied in the Children Act 1989 and the UN Convention.

6.29 Health Authorities have now developed a local strategy for health for each County in Wales which cover each health gain area and contain a separate chapter on services for children drawing on the guidance referred to above.

Infant Mortality

6.30 Although some regional variation has been noted, which may have been influenced by demographic, social and other factors, the infant mortality rate for England and Wales has again fallen. Between 1978 and 1992 the rate fell from 13.1 to 6.6 deaths per 1,000 live births - the lowest rate ever achieved. In Scotland in the same period it fell from 12.9 to 6.8 deaths per thousand. Targets for reducing accidental deaths in children and young people were included in the Government's Health Promotion strategy because accidents are the most common cause of death in children over age one. Encouraging progress is being made. Mortality figures for 1992 show that 9.0% of the 33% reduction sought for children under 15 and 4.8% of the 25% reduction sought for young people 15 to 24 has been achieved.

Primary Health Care

6.31 Deprived area payments have been introduced to increase the availability of family doctor services in the areas where needs are greatest. Child Health Surveillance (CHS) services have been made more accessible: over 90% of family doctors are now eligible to provide this service as part of integrated family health care. In Scotland about 67% of family doctors are eligible to provide such services providing child health surveillance to 66.5% of patients under 5.

Disease

6.32 Immunisation cover for infectious diseases in childhood is at record levels and the incidence of these diseases has shown a commensurate decrease.

Nutrition

6.33 A study of child nutrition shows that the average height of primary school children has increased in each of the last eight years. A Nutrition Task Force has been set up following publication of "Health of the Nation". It is considering how best to implement the nutrition targets set out in Health of the Nation, within the context of improving the whole diet and is looking at school meals, food and nutrition education in schools and the effects of food advertising on children. The Welfare Food Scheme continues to provide a nutritional safeguard by ensuring the provision of liquid milk, dried baby-milk and vitamin supplements to pregnant women, nursing mothers and children under 5 in families with low incomes.

Acute Care

6.34 Advances in medical science offer new opportunities in the acute care of children. A recent report by a working party convened by the British Paediatric Association shows that critically ill children are most appropriately treated in paediatric intensive care units and makes recommendations on the number and distribution of these units required to take account of developments in this specialised area of child health care. Health authorities have been asked to draw up plans for an effective and coordinated response to this report.

Child Health Surveillance

6.35 The UK is unique in having a long established programme of child health surveillance and family support, with health care being delivered by the primary health care team. This comprises doctors and community nurses (health visitors). The team arranges a combination of home visiting and visits to clinics, both in a community setting and on General Practitioners' premises.

6.36 The midwife starts the process through being involved during pregnancy. This involvement may continue until the 28th day following the birth of the baby as part of the midwives' statutory obligation. After this the health visitor becomes involved.

6.37 One of the health visitor's main responsibilities is to help ensure that infants have a healthy start in life. They may become involved with the family during pregnancy or shortly after the birth of the child - usually about the tenth day after the birth. They visit the family home to offer help and information about feeding, general health and safety and the infant's need for stimulation and normal child development.

6.38 A structured programme of child health surveillance is initiated comprising a series of checks for health, growth and development. Checks are scheduled during the first two weeks and again at 6-8 weeks. A primary course of immunisation takes place at 2, 3 and 4 months. Further physical examinations and tests are undertaken between 6-9 months, at 18-24 months, at 36-48 months, followed by a pre-school check at 54-66 months.

Child Health Records

6.39 Personal Child Health Records which record the health and development of children in the pre-school years are widely used. This form of record keeping has been promoted because of evidence to show that it encourages a helpful and informed partnership between parents, children and health professionals.

Nursing Children

6.40 Children in the UK have the advantage of being nursed within the National Health Service by specially trained nurses some of whom have further qualifications in advanced nursing.

Healthy Teeth

6.41   Dental Health Services are provided free to all children under 18. The following tables show the tooth/ bone decay experience of four age groups of the child and young adult population in England and Wales and three groups in Scotland recorded at different times in surveys. Compound annual reduction rates between the observation times are also shown. DMFT = Decayed/ Missing/ Filled Teeth. DFT = Decayed/ Filled teeth. In Scotland, dental health is recognised as a priority area and targets for dental health improvement have been set in its health strategy document, including one for 5 year olds.

England and Wales						
Age	Caries Index	Year of Survey	Survey Type	Base No.	Weighted Mean	Compound Annual Reduction Rate, %
5	dmft	1973 1983 1989/90	OPCS OPCS BASCD	952 719 163,814	4.0 1.8 1.7	7.7 0.9
12	dmft	1973 1983 1988/89	OPCS OPCS BASCD	956 1,036 101,294	4.8 2.9 1.5	4.9 11.3
14	dmft	1973 1983 1986/87	OPCS OPCS BASCD	923 1,109 38,889	7.4 4.7 3.4	4.4 8.8
16-24	dmft	1968 1978 1988	OPCS OPCS BASCD	375 567 622	15.8 14.5 10.4	4.9 11.3

Scotland					
Age	Caries Index	Year of Survey	Survey Type	Base No.	Weighted Mean
5	dft dft dmft dft dmft dft dmft	1983 1987/88 1989/90 1991/92	OPCS SHBDEP SHBDEP SHBDEP	319 4472 4401 5001	3.2 2.22 2.73 2.23 2.82 2.34 2.88
12	dmft dmft dmft	1983 1988/89 1992/93	OPCS SHBDEP SHBDEP	525 3818 5344	4.5 2.23 2.08
14	dmft dmft	1983 1990/91	OPCS SHBDEP	588 3419	6.8 3.55

School Health Service

6.42 Long standing provisions for school health services were reinforced in the 1944 Education Act which imposed on local authorities the duty to provide medical inspections for children in all maintained primary and secondary schools, and to secure for them all forms of medical and dental treatment free of charge. These services were transferred from local education authority control to the NHS in 1974 during reorganisation. School and pre-school health care is now evolving into a community based fully integrated service for all children

Traditional Practices

6.43 The Prohibition of Female Circumcision Act 1985 makes it an offence to carry out any procedures which are known as female circumcision but which are more accurately described as female genital mutilation (FGM). The Act also makes it illegal to aid, abet, counsel or procure the carrying out of these procedures. Further legal protection is provided by the Children Act 1989. Guidance was issued in October 1991 to all local authorities, health authorities, the police, the probation service, schools, doctors and a wide range of voluntary organisations working in the child care field, containing advice on the 1985 Act and on dealing with FGM. The Government funds an organisation called FORWARD which works to educate the relevant communities and the professionals concerned about FGM.

Environmental Pollution factors

Pesticides

6.44 In the UK infants and children are recognised as a special group needing careful consideration. Their less developed systems may mean that for some pesticides they can be more susceptible to toxicity from intake of a pesticide and for others they may be less susceptible than adults. The special vulnerability, if any, of infants to a particular chemical substance is taken into account when Acceptable Daily Intakes (ADI) are determined. Pesticides are not approved for use if even those who eat a more than average amount of treated produce would have intakes of the pesticide above the ADI which is an internationally agreed safety level. Food consumed by infants and children is monitored routinely by the Government's Working Party on Pesticide Residues. All results are published annually.

6.45 The Independent Advisory Committee on Pesticides saw an executive summary of the US report on pesticides in the diets of infants and children at its meeting on 8 July 1993. The Committee agreed that the report should be considered in detail and a further paper will be submitted to the Committee in 1994.

Clean Drinking water

6.46 Drinking water in the UK is of a very high quality and is safe to drink. Rigorous quality standards are set in national legislation, in some cases going beyond those in the European Community Drinking Water Directive. These standards are strictly and effectively enforced. The European Commission is currently reviewing the Drinking Water Directive. The review may be expected to have regard to the soon to be published WHO recommendations for drinking water quality.

Clean Air

6.47 The Clean Air Acts of 1956 and 1968 have reduced emissions from chimneys markedly. The Environmental Protection Act 1990 has introduced Integrated Pollution Control to force cleaner technology and has given local authorities new powers to control pollution from less complex plant.

Traffic and Environmental pollution

6.48 EC Directive 91/441/EEC, which came into effect in UK law on 31 December 1992, sets tighter limits on emissions of carbon monoxide, hydrocarbons and oxides of nitrogen (NOx) by new cars and light vans. Diesel cars additionally must comply with a strict limit on particulates (smoke). Directive 93/59/EEC, which came into effect on 1 October 1993, further reduces emission limits for light vans to a level of similar technical severity as that mandated for cars.

6.49 The limits in effect require new petrol-engined cars to use three-way catalytic converters which can only function with unleaded petrol. This will undoubtedly reinforce the present trend for increasing use of unleaded petrol - currently 53% of all petrol sales - which is attributable to measures taken by the Government to gradually increase the duty differential between leaded and unleaded petrol and to the requirement for all new cars manufactured from October 1990 to be capable of running on unleaded petrol.

6.50 Stricter limits for new diesel-engined trucks and buses over 3.5 tonnes, which were set by directive 91/542/EEC, are being introduced for the same gaseous pollutants in two stages. The first, in October 1993, substantially reduces the limit for emissions of NOx and establishes limits for particulate emissions. The second, 1996 stage, goes further with NOx reduction, so that the limit value will be less than half its present value, and reduces the particulate limit value to a level of stringency similar to that to be applied in the United States from 1994.

6.51 As a result of these measures a progressive reduction in regulated pollutants is expected as the vehicle fleet is replaced.

6.52 In addition, the UK and its EC partners recently adopted a common position on EC proposals for further measures to be applied to cars and vans in 1996 which will enable further reductions of 20% and 50% in the limit values of carbon monoxide and hydrocarbons/oxides of nitrogen. Additional measures are to be applied to all classes of vehicle by the year 2000.

6.53 Checking vehicle emissions levels in statutory annual roadworthiness tests is another key element of the government's strategy for controlling pollution and improving air quality. Metered smoke and emissions checks are now made on most vehicles and it is proposed to reintroduce them for diesel engined cars and vans from February 1994. The emission levels which vehicles have to meet are to be reduced in accordance with directive 92/95EEC.

6.54 On carbon dioxide emissions, the UK has assisted in the provision of an amending EC directive which provides an agreed method of measurement of CO_2 emissions from all vehicles. This is the precursor to a further directive which is being considered by the Commission to introduce a system that will encourage the reduction of CO_2 emissions from vehicles. In the meantime the Government is committed to sustained real increases in both petrol and diesel prices to encourage better fuel economy measures from the motoring public.

Child Road Safety - Targets

6.55 Targets to reduce casualties by one-third by the year 2,000 (based on 1981-85 average) were set out in the 1987 Inter-Departmental Review on Road Safety 'Road Safety - The Next Steps'. Progress in achieving the target for lowering numbers of children killed or seriously injured has been encouraging and the UK statistics for the 12 months to June 1993 are as follows:-

Latest 1993 figures	0-4	5-7	8-11	12-15	TOTAL
Pedestrians	685	941	1400	1471	4497
Cyclists	25	161	376	603	1165
Car passengers	295	197	303	512	1307
Other Categories	27	23	54	150	254
81-85 baseline	1380	2027	3501	4773	11681
% reduction	25.2%	34.8%	39.1%	42.7%	38.2%

6.56 All child road accident casualties have reduced by 15% compared to the 1981-85 average. 1992 figures reveal a continuing success with child pedestrian deaths which are now 53% below the baseline average.

Strategy

6.57 The strategy set out in 'Children and Roads: A Safer Way', as with the Government's strategy for tackling road accidents generally, envisages an approach on 3 main fronts:

i   enforcement (legislation)

ii   education (including publicity)

iii   engineering (roads and vehicles).

Enforcement

6.58 The law relating to the use of seat belts or child restraints in vehicles was further tightened in February 1993. It is now illegal to carry a child under 14 years old unrestrained in the front seat of any vehicle and children under three years of age travelling in the front seat must be carried in a child restraint appropriate to their weight. Children in the rear of a car must wear seat belts or appropriate child restraints wherever available and if one is available in the front but not the rear, they must (if under 12 years and under 150cm in height) sit in the front of the vehicle.

6.59 The Road Traffic Act 1991 made it easier for the police to prosecute drivers for bad driving and introduced the offence of 'causing death by dangerous driving and causing death by careless driving when under the influence of drink or drugs'. On 16 August 1993 the maximum sentence for this offence was increased from five to ten years. Drivers convicted of the dangerous driving offences must now pass a double length driving test, following disqualification, before they can be reissued with a full driving licence. Courts may also order drivers disqualified for other serious driving offences, or on penalty points, to take a double length test.

6.60 In August 1993 the Government launched a consultation paper on new driver safety. The aim is to improve new driver knowledge, behaviour and perception of risks and will involve changes to the driver training and testing regime with a mixture of enforcement and education measures. The Department of Transport is currently considering the responses to the consultation which ended on 1 November 1993. The document includes a proposal to require newly qualified drivers who commit offences to re-take the driving test.

Safety Education

6.61 The Department for Transport works closely with the Department for

Education and they have established an inter Departmental working group to advise on the educational research programme. Scottish Development Department, Welsh Office, Northern Ireland Office are also represented on this group.

6.62 Guidance for primary and secondary school teachers on how to deliver road safety education in the classroom within the framework of the national curriculum is to be produced in the next few months, following extensive testing in two local authorities (Sheffield and Hertfordshire). The British Institute of Traffic Education Research (BITER), in collaboration with road safety officers, is developing an approach to road safety education for trainee teachers which aims to ensure that they are both well-equipped and motivated to teach road safety within the national curriculum.

6.63 A computer data base of national curriculum based road safety material for road safety practitioners and/or teachers is being developed as part of our research programme. This will include material developed by the Royal Society for the Prevention of Accidents (RoSPA), the British Institute of Traffic Education Research (BITER) and Road Safety Officers many of whom also develop their own material.

6.64 A new programme of pedestrian training for 5 to 8 year olds has been launched around the country, based on a project in training young children being undertaken in Strathclyde. Some local authorities already have pedestrian training schemes. RoSPA are reviewing pedestrian training schemes to identify good practice and prepare guidance for local authorities.

6.65 The consultation document on the safety of newly qualified drivers proposes the implementation of an expanded programme of road safety education directed at the 16 + age group. Research has been commissioned in support of the development of that programme.

Publicity

6.66 The Government's "Kill your Speed. Not a Child" campaign has been running since October 1991. Research shows a growing awareness of the message that, in an accident, a vehicle's reduced speed can greatly influence a child's chance of survival but so far drivers are not acting on the message. A further phase of the campaign was launched in September 1993 reinforcing the message that drivers should slow down when children are likely to be about.

6.67 Other publicity activity aimed at child safety includes the 'Cycle Safe' campaign, covering a broad range of cycling safety issues and aimed primarily at older children and younger teenagers. This has featured a television commercial encouraging children to wear cycle helmets. Also on the subject of cycle helmets, Customs and Excise have recently ruled that cycle helmets may be zero-rated for VAT purposes provided that they are for sale specifically to children and have a maximum circumference of 59cm. Customs and Excise believe that this is a generous limit which will afford relief to the great majority of children.

Private Sector

6.68 Launched on the same day as 'Children and Roads. A Safer Way' was a pilot Traffic Club for pre-school children. This was sponsored by an insurance company, General Accident in the eastern region of England. It aimed to ensure as many children as possible aged 3-5 get structured traffic education from their parents - some 75,000 children enrolled. After research showed encouraging signs that the pilot scheme was proving beneficial, the scheme was launched nationally on 10 June 93.

6.69 Kwik Fit, a motor repair chain ran a seat belt TV campaign to tie in with the Government's seat belt campaign in February 1993. Some thirty companies, organisations and other interested parties have contributed to, or pledged an involvement in the Department of Transport's 'Cycle Safe' campaign. Halfords, a motor spares chain, supported the campaign by running a national competition on cereal packets. Bell, a protective headgear manufacturer, sponsored the showing on satellite television of the Department's commercial to persuade children to wear cycle helmets.

6.70 BP's "Living with Traffic" initiative and long standing road safety teams take road safety teaching into schools all over the country and provide teaching resources linked to the National Curriculum.

6.71 Texaco have supported the "Kill your Speed. Not a Child" campaign through television commercials and, more recently, forecourt posters and local road safety initiatives. Further private sector contributions include Great Universal Stores, Volvo, Volkswagen, Britax and a number of cycle helmet manufacturers.

Engineering

6.72 The UK is responsible for initiating the move within Europe to make the fronts of cars less harmful to pedestrians, cyclists and motorcyclists in the event of a collision. The Department of Transport is co-operating in the drafting of an appropriate EC Directive in this respect. Manufacturers are already incorporating in their cars some of the measures that are being proposed in the Directive and this initiative will continue to be encouraged.

6.73 Government guidance was issued in February 1993 giving greater flexibility to Local Traffic Authorities (LTAs) on the setting of speed limits. This allowed a move away from accidents as the main determining factor and placed more stress on the environment through which a road passes.

6.74 A document "Killing Speed / Saving Lives" issued in January 1993 set out the Department of Transport's accident policy on speed across the board and gave specific advice on 20mph zones. Nearly seventy such zones have now been approved. There is evidence that they have been especially effective in reducing child pedestrian casualties (by up to 80% in some areas) and total casualties in some zones have been reduced by over 50%.

6.75   The UK's transport policy gives full consideration to the rights of all groups in society, including children. This includes measures to reduce the impact of transport on the environment, in particular through reduced emissions from road vehicles. We are also investing a great deal in public transport. In 1992/93, spending in this area amounted to around £3 billion. British Rail investment amounted to 1.4 billion last year. This is the highest investment since the early 1960s.

The National Travel Survey

6.76   The 1989/91 National Travel Survey report shows tables including journeys under one mile except where their presence may distort the results. The survey gives as much prominence to education journeys as to commuting journeys and it is one of the few national travel surveys in the world which collects information on journeys made by children of all ages, including those aged under 3 years old.

Roads

6.77   A major objective of the roads programme is to take traffic away from town and village centres, separating it from pedestrians, cyclists and all vulnerable road users including children.

6.78   Traffic calming measures in towns and villages are designed to make those areas safer for all vulnerable road users, including children. The Traffic Calming Act which came into effect on 16 May 1992 provides powers for the Secretary of State to make regulations and specially authorise traffic calming works. The Regulations came into effect on 27 August 1993 and all local authorities have been advised through the issue of Circulars on Roads and Traffic Advisory leaflets.

6.79   The Government is well aware of the importance of cycling as an aid to the personal mobility of young people and aims to make conditions for cyclists safer and more attractive. Apart from the continuing programme of road safety publicity and education aimed at improving road users' awareness and behaviour, we have been encouraging local authorities to make proper provision for cyclists. We undertake a wide range of research to develop better facilities for cycling and issue extensive guidance to local authorities and other providers on legal, planning and design issues. This covers such areas as the provision of cycle routes, cycle lanes and secure cycle parking.

6.80 We accept that "appropriate assistance" should be given "to parents and legal guardians in the performance of their child rearing responsibilities" (Article 18.2). Listed below are just some of the measures taken by British Rail (BR) to make it easier for parents and guardians with young children to travel by train. Several main line stations have facilities for nursing mothers and their babies and some of the more modern rolling stock on Network South East, Regional Railways and InterCity have nappy changing facilities in some toilets.

6.81 During school holidays InterCity provide free "fun packs" which are available from the buffet section of trains. These packs contain a story book, a colouring book, pencils and badges, and are designed to keep children amused during long journeys.

6.82 We also believe that it is important to educate children about safety on the railways. In 1991, BR launched its Railway Code which aims to educate both adults and children on what they can do to avoid unnecessary risks on the railways and how to improve their own safety. A version of the Code for younger children, Roald Dahl's Guide to Railway Safety, was also published by BR in 1991.

6.83 Talks are given to children in their schools by BR drivers and British Transport Police as part of BR's safety campaign. BR are determined to reduce the toll of death and injury to trespassers on the railway which is still the biggest cause of fatalities and casualties on the tracks.

6.84 BR have also produced 2 videos to complement their talks in schools. 'Only Fools Break the Rules' is aimed at 6-11 year olds and teaches them how to enjoy travelling by train safely, but warns of the dangers of playing on railway lines, particularly the unseen dangers of electrified rails and overhead power cables.

6.85 'Killing Time' is the most graphic safety video ever produced by BR. The hard hitting programme is for children aged between 12 and 16 and opens with a group of bored youngsters who decide to play 'chicken' on the railway - with fatal consequences. The programme contains harrowing interviews with train drivers, some of whose trains have run down and killed trespassers, and with police officers who have cleared up in the aftermath.

6.86 A recent Health and Safety Executive report on rail safety noted that child fatalities among trespassers on the railway had fallen from 15 in 1991/92 to only 5 in 1992/93.

6.87 BR do provide discounted fares for children and we expect private operators will do the same.

Buses

6.88 Facilities at bus stations are a matter for the operator(s) of the bus station. This could either be the local authority or the bus company. Therefore, with regard to facilities for children and babies, this has always been a matter for the owners of the bus stations. Whilst we recognise the importance of such facilities, we have no powers to ensure that they are provided at bus stations. However, many bus and coach stations do have reasonable facilities including baby changing rooms.

Overseas Aid

6.89 Article 24.4 is fully endorsed in the work of the British Aid Programme. It is recognised that in many societies, children do not have ready access to health care. Malnutrition and infections are the primary causes of death among children. Many more become permanently disabled. A high proportion of these deaths can be prevented if the right services are available. Because children are so vulnerable, it is important that they are given priority within the National Primary health Care Strategies. In addition, the UK seeks to ensure, through its health assistance programmes, that overseas governments are made fully aware of the specific needs of children when implementing their health programmes. Work undertaken by the Overseas Development Administration in India involves children in health education, and these messages are passed from children, through their parents, into the community. Other initiatives include a mother and child health project in an area of India covering 25 million people.

Social Security and child care services and facilities - Articles 26 and 18, para 3 and Standard of living - Article 27, paras 1-3

Social Security

6.90 Through the Social Security system, the Government provides a comprehensive system of financial support and assistance to families with children. The cornerstone of the system is Child Benefit, a universal non means-tested, non-contributory benefit which is payable at a flat rate in respect of each child, with (since 1991) a higher rate for the first child. This benefit is normally paid to the mother as the primary carer for the child. A person bringing up a child alone is entitled to an additional amount of benefit for the family.

6.91 The Government have taken particular steps in recent years to focus additional Social Security help on lower-income families with children. Reform of the Social Security system in 1988 put in place a revised structure which enabled financial help to be focused more effectively on families, both out of work and in work. In 1993/94 this meant that around £1 billion extra could be made available to lower-income families, compared with the position before 1988. The real disposable income of all types of families with children is now on average appreciably higher than in 1979.

6.92 Child Benefit is paid to all families, and additional benefits are paid in many cases to recipients of contributory Social Security benefits who have dependent children. There is also a special benefit payable to those who assume the care of an orphan. However, the main help with general living expenses for low income families with children is through Income Support, an income-related benefit payable to people who work less than 16 hours a week and whose income, from all sources, is below a level approved each year by Parliament. An allowance according to age is paid in respect of each child and a flat-rate additional premium is paid for each family. Income Support is complemented by a system of income-related help with housing and with local taxation, which again is geared to family size and age of children.

6.93 The Social Fund helps with specific expenses in exceptional circumstances.

6.94 An important feature of UK help for families with children is Family Credit, introduced in 1988. This is an income-related Social Security benefit for employed or self-employed people with children, who work 16 or more hours a week. This extra financial help is payable to couples and lone parents and enables low income working families to improve their standard of living by a combination of wages and benefits. An improvement to Family Credit to be introduced from October 1994 will provide additional help with childcare costs. This will further improve the value of the benefit to working families and increase the incentive for many unemployed families to be better off in work.

6.95 The Government's policy towards young people involves training, education and employment, with support for vulnerable youngsters through the benefit system. The aim is to provide young people aged 16-17 with the opportunity Youth Training provides, not to have them begin adult life dependent on benefits. Some young people who are unable to take part in training can get Income Support, such as lone parents and people with disabilities. The severe hardship provision allows financial support to be given to young people in or at risk of hardship until a job or YT place is secured. This provision works - over 85% of those currently applying receive Income Support and on average the percentage is even higher for rough sleepers, care leavers and pregnant young women.

6.96 Although Great Britain and Northern Ireland have largely separate administrative and legal provision for social security, the Northern Ireland social security system operates in parity with the remainder of the United Kingdom.

Day Care

6.97 In the field of day care, the Government recognises that we need to build on the achievements that have been made in increasing the number of day nurseries and child minders figures for which are set out earlier in this report. The Children Act gives local authorities in England and Wales a strategic function for day care services in their area. Every three years they are required to review the pattern of provision, the process preferably involving consultation with local organisations and individuals,and to publish a report. This provision gives a framework for coherent development and expansion. The Department of Health and the Welsh Office are monitoring the impact of this new duty, through an evaluation project and analysis of a sample of reports. The Government is also using funds to pump prime an expansion of day care services for school age children. The Central Community Relations Unit in Northern Ireland supported recent research which included a study of models of cross-community child care. In Northern Ireland, following an inter-departmental review, a new policy statement, which will form the basis for the future development of day care services is to be published early in 1994. Its principles are consistent with the UN Convention.

6.98 The Department of Health is funding, over 3 years, 12 posts based in voluntary organisations to develop services in different parts of the country. The Employment Department and the Welsh Office are running a programme over a number of years involving Training and Enterprise Councils in dispersing monies to organisations to set up new schemes. The aim of this programme is to improve the level and service and thus make it easier for parents to go back into the job market.

After-school care

6.99 The UK Government has been taking steps to promote improvements in child care provision, including provision for the children of working parents. As part of this initiative, the Department for Education wrote to all publicly maintained schools in England in October 1989 asking them to consider what they could do to encourage more use of school premises for after school care. This was followed up in June 1992 by a further letter from the Minister of State for Education, in which schools were again urged to consider opening up their premises for child care schemes where there was local demand for such provision.

Nursery Education

6.100   The UK Government has made it clear that it would like to see a widening of nursery and other pre-school education as resources become available. The longer-term ambition is universal availability for those who want it. Much has already been achieved. Over half of three and four year olds now attend maintained nursery and primary schools, and more than

90% receive some form of pre-school provision. The Government intends to explore ways of adding still further, as resources allow, to the choice parents have among the range of provision - public, private and voluntary. As well as encouraging this choice and diversity in response to children's needs and parents' preferences and circumstances, the Government will continue to promote quality and cost-effectiveness.

Chapter 7: Education, Leisure and Cultural Activities

Education, including vocational training and guidance - Article 28

7.1   The aim of education in the UK is to develop to the full the talents of both children and adults - for their own benefit and that of society as a whole. Children must by law receive education between the ages of 5 (4 in Northern Ireland) and 16. Well over 90% go to publicly financed schools, generically known as State schools, the rest attend private schools. About 53% of 3 and 4 year old children go to school and over 70% of 16 year olds now choose to remain in full-time education, in school or a further education college, for another one or two years before seeking employment, undertaking training on a Government scheme or entering higher education.

7.2   Although the overall approach to education is now broadly similar throughout the UK, the service is administered separately in England, Wales, Scotland and Northern Ireland.

Policies and objectives

7.3   A series of reforms has been introduced during the last few years to implement the principal objectives of the Government's education policies. These objectives include:

   i   to raise standards of attainment at all ability levels;

   ii   to increase parental choice and improve partnerships between parents and schools;

   iii   to increase autonomy and accountability of schools and colleges;

   iv   to implement a broader and more balanced curriculum designed to develop the qualities and skills needed in adult and working life;

   v   to increase and widen participation in post-16 education and training and to make it more economically relevant;

   vi   to obtain good value for money from the education service as a whole.

Equal Opportunities

7.4   By setting out statutory learning objectives and programmes of study in ten subjects, the National Curriculum in England and Wales will ensure that all pupils, regardless of their sex, receive a broad and balanced education to the age of 16. Both boys and girls will gain essential skills and knowledge in subjects which, traditionally, have been perceived to be oriented towards one sex and, as a result, should be able to make informed decisions about a wide range of opportunities in education, training and employment at the end of their school career. The Scottish Consultative Committee on the Curriculum has updated guidance on equal opportunities and has published and issued to all Scottish schools, on 18 October 1993, 2 booklets promoting a positive approach to equal opportunities throughout all school activities. This is reinforced by the 5-14 Programme guidelines issued by The Scottish Office Education Department.

Article 28.1. (a)

7.5   Both primary and secondary education in the UK is compulsory and available free to all.

Article 28. 1. (b) Different forms of secondary education

7.6   The Government encourages the development of choice and diversity in secondary education to enhance parental choice and provide appropriate opportunities for children.

CTCs, TSI and Technology Colleges

7.7   Under the Education Reform Act 1988 some 15 City Technology Colleges (CTCs) have been established in urban areas around the country. These schools are a partnership between Government and the Private Sector, with the private sector responsible for their governance. CTCs provide a full secondary education, based on the National Curriculum, but with a curriculum bias towards technology, science and mathematics.   All children within the large catchment areas are eligible to apply and the schools accept pupils across the full range of ability.

7.8   The Technology Schools Initiative (TSI) was launched in December 1991. Its aim was to establish a network of secondary schools committed to providing technology and associated courses of a strongly vocational nature, and eventually to disseminate the experience of TSI to all schools. 222 schools have been given TSI awards to enable them to enhance their facilities for technology teaching.

7.9   Building on the experience of CTCs and the TSI, the Government is now encouraging secondary schools around the country to become Technology Colleges. Technology Colleges will provide the National

Curriculum but in addition will emphasise technology, science and mathematics. They will involve a partnership between the Government and the private sector, with the latter nominating governors to be included on the school's governing body. The first Technology Colleges will begin operating in 1994.

7.10 CTCs, TSI schools and Technology Colleges all offer free education.

Vocational Education

7.11 The National Curriculum in England and Wales covers important prevocational skills. The basic and core skills are taught throughout, and all National Curriculum subjects, particularly technology, are designed to be taught in real contexts.

7.12 Vocational awarding bodies are developing new vocational options for children under 16 years of age, some of which were piloted last year. The Government has ensured that the curriculum requirements for 14-16 year olds are flexible enough to allow schools to offer units towards these vocational qualifications. It has also provided funds under its 1994-95 Grants for Education Support and Training programme to help schools offer more vocational options. There will be close cooperation between the School Curriculum and Assessment Authority and the National Council for Vocational Qualifications (NCVQ) to ensure that high quality GNVQ options can be introduced into schools as an established and well respected part of the 14-16 school curriculum.

7.13 After age 16 the Government is introducing three qualifications pathways: general education, general vocational qualifications and job specific vocational qualifications. These three types of qualifications will increasingly be available and accessible to every child.

Further Education Funding and Participation

7.14 The Government is committed to increasing the participation rate of 16-18 year olds in further education, and to improving their levels of attainment. To help achieve those aims, the Government has introduced major changes in the organisation and funding of further education.

7.15 Further education and sixth form colleges have been given independent status, and brought together in a new and coherent sector of further education funded by new national funding councils for England and for Wales. These councils have a statutory duty to secure adequate provision of further education for the population of their areas.

7.16 Colleges in the new sector have been given a strong financial incentive to recruit and retain more students. That should ensure increased recruitment, and improved standards of delivery. Colleges may not charge tuition fees for 16-18 year old home and EC students on full-time courses; other students may be charged fees, but colleges are free to remit or reduce fees in case of need.

7.17 Record numbers of 16 and 17 year olds are already participating in full-time further education in England: an estimated 71% of 16 year olds, and 55% of 17 year olds (FE and schools) in 1992- 93.

7.18 Nevertheless, the Government is committed to increasing 16-18 year old participation still further. The Government's spending plans announced in autumn 1993, which provide for a 25% increase in student numbers in further education over the next 3 years, will help lift the UK towards the top of the international league table for staying on rates for 16-18 year olds.

28. 1. (c) Access to Higher Education

7.19 The UK Government remains committed to the principle that higher education (HE) should be available to those who are suitably qualified and motivated to benefit from it. Public funding has been increased rapidly in the last few years to facilitate the expansion of higher education. Participation by young people in Great Britain has reached the record level of about 30%. Near parity has been achieved between the numbers of men and women home full-time students.

7.20 Arrangements for student support, which are among the most generous in the world, ensure that those from poorer families have access to higher education. Virtually all full-time students have their tuition fees paid in full and receive a means-tested grant. They are also eligible for a non-means tested loan. Disabled students are eligible for extra payments. Access funds totalling £26m for England alone are available to help students in particular financial difficulty.

7.21 The Higher Education Funding Councils for England, Wales and Scotland are all considering how they can encourage wider access. The Higher Education Funding Council for England has set aside £3m in 1993/94 to improve access for students with special educational needs, and a further £0.5m to encourage ethnic minority recruitment to initial teacher training.

7.22 Guidance and information on HE courses is available from a variety of sources including advisory services within schools and further education colleges. Higher education institutions provide comprehensive information, which is widely available in schools, colleges and public libraries, about the courses and facilities they provide. The Department for Education publishes guidance on an annual basis about student grants and loans.

Careers Education

7.23 The National Curriculum provides a foundation for all future educational and vocational choices.

7.24 Non-statutory guidance on how careers education and guidance might develop over the years of compulsory schooling was published by the National Curriculum Council in 1990.

7.25 All pupils may expect to receive individual guidance at age 15 - 16. To ensure that it shall be of good quality, the Government has boosted school careers libraries, encouraged close links between careers specialists inside and outside of the schools, provided aids for staff training, and fostered the involvement of employers in a variety of ways; and so, for example, nearly all pupils now receive work experience at 15.

7.26 The quality of careers work is monitored, notably by the Office for Standards in Education as part of their overall programme of inspection of schools.

Information about Further Education

7.27 The Secretary of State for Education has made regulations under Section 50 of the FHE Act 1992 requiring FE colleges in England and Wales to publish information on the educational achievements of their students and their subsequent career routes.

7.28 The publication of information under Section 50 will enable prospective students, parents, employers and other interested parties, to be better informed when making decisions about post-16 education, through the availability on a local level of:

i   detailed information on students' examination results in A levels and AS;

ii   comprehensive information on students' achievements in General National Vocational Qualifications (GNVQs), National Vocational Qualifications (NVQs) and other vocational qualifications;

iii   information on the routes taken by students having achieved their qualifications.

Information published will assist prospective students and parents to make judgements about the quality of provision in a college, and how it compares with that of other colleges and other types of institution post-16.

National Performance Tables

7.29 The Government is also, for the first time, publishing comparative information on the performance of all institutions offering education and training to 16-18 year olds. The performance tables will include information about both academic and vocational qualifications and will cover colleges in the further education sector and schools.

Further Education Charter

7.30 A Charter for Further Education was issued in September 1993. The Charter will ensure high standards of service for all those who use further education by setting challenging standards for the delivery of key services. All colleges in the further education sector will also have to develop their own charters by summer 1994 within the framework of the national Charter. These charters will cover local needs and priorities, and set specific standards for the provision of services by individual colleges.

28. 1. (e) Attendance

7.31 The Government attaches considerable importance to regular school attendance by pupils of compulsory school age. To help those schools experiencing difficulty in maintaining high levels of attendance, the Department for Education is supporting projects to a total value of some £9.6m in 71 English local education authorities (LEAs) under the "Reducing Truancy" category of the Grants for Education Support and Training (GEST) Scheme for 1993 - 94.

7.32 The Department for Education has also funded a major research project on the scale and nature of truancy in English secondary schools. The one-year investigation was carried out by a team from the University of North London and involved some 150 LEA-maintained secondary schools and over 37,000 pupils in years 10 and 11 (age range 14-16). Advance copies of the project report were published on 25 June 1993.

7.33 Under education law, LEAs are legally responsible for enforcing regular school attendance where pupils of compulsory school age are concerned. This function is normally carried out by education welfare officers (EWOs) employed by LEAs. The Department for Education is currently supporting EWO training in the areas of educational disadvantage and parental participation through grants to a total of some £15,000 to the Education Welfare Service's Training Advisory Group. EWO activity (including the appointment of additional staff) is also supported by the GEST scheme referred to above.

7.34 Since 1991 schools have been required by Government regulations to distinguish in their morning and afternoon registers between authorised and unauthorised absence. In November 1993 information on levels of unauthorised absence appeared for the first time in the school performance tables published pursuant to the Government's Parent's Charter. The aim of these measures is to encourage schools to pay greater attention to unauthorised absence - whether straight truancy or parentally-condoned unjustified absence - and to ensure that parents have access to attendance data for schools in their area.

Discipline

7.35 The question of discipline in schools was considered in detail by an independent Committee of Enquiry set up in March 1988 and chaired by Lord Elton. The Committee's report was published a year later and was welcomed by the Government. Copies were distributed by the Department for Education to all schools and LEAs in England. Recommendation 27 in the Report - addressed to head teachers and teachers - recommended that punishments which humiliate pupils should be avoided.

7.36 On 4 January 1994 the Department for Education issued a consultation package entitled "Pupils with Problems". Document 1 in the package is concerned with pupil behaviour and discipline.

Corporal Punishment

7.37 Corporal punishment in maintained schools in England and Wales was abolished by the Education (No.2) Act 1986. The ban also extends to publicly funded pupils in independent schools in England and Wales . The Government has decided that, on grounds of parental choice, corporal punishment should remain available for privately funded pupils in independent schools. The Education Act 1993 now expressly provides that corporal punishment in schools must not be inhuman or degrading.

28. 3. International co-operation

7.38 The Department for Education has a wide range of links with Education Ministries in other countries. Bi-lateral activities range from informal exchanges of ideas and experience on policy developments within the education field to large-scale bi-lateral Colloquia to promote educational exchanges and support the teaching of each other's language in the partner country. Formal programmes have been agreed with several European partners to further develop and extend bi-lateral cooperation in education.

7.39 In a multi-lateral context, the UK participates actively in the EC Education Committee, although, until the Maastricht Treaty was ratified, the main focus of the Committee's work was at post-school level. The UK has welcomed the LINGUA programme's support for Teacher Training in modern foreign languages, which gives Community support to activities designed to improve language teaching in the UK.

7.40 The UK is also an active participant in the Education Committees of the Council of Europe and OECD, much of whose work focuses on the encouragement of international co-operation in matters relating to education.

7.41   International cooperation in education is promoted through the Central Bureau for Educational Visits and Exchanges (CBEVE) which is funded by the Department for Education (DFE), the Scottish Office Education Department (SOED) and the Department of Education Northern Ireland (DENI)

7.42   The principal aim of the CBEVE is to improve educational provision in the UK by promoting and supporting the international dimension throughout the curriculum in all sectors of the education system; the teaching and learning of modern foreign languages.

7.43   The UK Government gives a high priority to the provision of education aid to developing countries. The Overseas Development Administration provides some kind of support to education in most of the countries with which it has programmes, with the greater part committed to Africa, but with substantial projects in India, Indonesia and other Asian countries.

Northern Ireland

7.44   In Northern Ireland an examination is underway in Training Schools about the desirability and demand for vocational education within the schools. Policy on discipline in these schools conforms with this Article.

Aims of education - Article 29

7.45   The Education Reform Act 1988 requires the school curriculum in maintained schools in England and Wales to promote the spiritual, moral, cultural, mental and physical development of pupils; and to prepare such pupils for the opportunities, responsibilities and experiences of adult life.

7.46   The Government has introduced a National Curriculum for pupils aged 5 to 16 in all maintained schools in England and Wales. The implementation of the National Curriculum is a very high priority for schools. The development of pupils' international understanding, preparation for a responsible life as members of a free society, and respect for the natural environment will be addressed primarily through the National Curriculum subjects.

7.47   The National Curriculum provides opportunities for pupils to develop an understanding of the world in which they live and of societies and civilisations different from their own through a range of subjects, but particularly through geography and history.

Respect for human rights

7.48   The National Curriculum in History requires that all children are taught about the origins of the United Nations, including the Universal Declaration of Human Rights.

Respect for cultural identity, etc

7.49 Following publication of the Report of the Committee of Inquiry into the Education of Children from Ethnic Minority Groups in March 1985 the then Secretary of State, Sir Keith Joseph, defined Government policy as being:

i   to raise the performance of all pupils and to tackle the obstacles to higher achievement which are common to all;

ii   to give ethnic minority pupils the same opportunity as all others to profit from what the schools can offer them, by meeting their particular educational needs, for example by promoting good practice in the teaching of English;

iii that schools should preserve and transmit our national values in a way which accepts Britain's ethnic diversity and promotes tolerance and racial harmony.

Citizenship

7.50 The Education Reform Act 1988 requires that the curriculum of every maintained school in England and Wales should prepare pupils for the opportunities, responsibilities and experiences of adult life.

7.51 The National Curriculum Council published non-statutory guidance in 1990 on the handling of Education for Citizenship. This includes a component on rights, duties and responsibilities. Governors and head teachers of schools are responsible for the detailed curricular arrangements.

7.52 Education for Citizenship will help to prepare pupils for responsible life in a free society by developing their understanding of the rights, duties and responsibilities of all citizens, whatever their ethnic, national or religious group. In Scotland, guidance has been in place for some time which has resulted in a system formally integrated into the staffing structure in schools' allocated promoted posts, and afforded time within the curriculum to cover Social/ Personal, Curricular and Careers guidance.

The natural environment

7.53 Environmental education provides opportunities for pupils to develop respect for the natural environment. One of the attainment targets in the National Curriculum Geography Order is devoted to environmental geography and requires study of a range of environmental issues, including whether certain types of environment might need special protection and the management of environments. Environmental issues also arise in the current statutory requirements for both science and technology.

Leisure, recreation and cultural activities - Article 31

Play

7.54 The Government acknowledges that good quality play facilities benefit children's all round development. Children aged under 5 and during their first years in school develop knowledge of themselves and the world around them through play. Older children need opportunities for play in order to develop wider interests and make good use of their leisure time, both as children and when they become adults. Voluntary organisations at national and local level are active in promoting play opportunities.

7.55 Support for children's play is channelled through a number of Government Departments. The Department of National Heritage has lead responsibility in England. The GB Sports Council, which it funds, runs a National Play and Information Centre, is developing playwork National Vocational Qualifications for those working with school aged children, grant-aids four National Centres for Playwork Education and, through its Trust Company, supports the National Voluntary Council for Children's Play. The Department also issues a guidance booklet on playground safety entitled 'Playground Safety Guidelines'.

7.56 The Department of the Environment supports local play provision and sporting provision for young people through the Revenue Support Grant, which it gives to English local authorities. Play projects in inner city areas are also supported through the Department's Urban Programme and City Challenge schemes.

7.57 In Wales, the Welsh Office provides funding for Play Wales which is hosted by the Council of Welsh Districts. This provides advice and support to local play providers in Wales. A similar function is performed by PlayBoard Northern Ireland. This is funded by the Youth Council for Northern Ireland which in turn is funded by the Department of Education for Northern Ireland.

7.58 The Department of Health grant aids several national organisations, which are active in this area. The Pre-school Playgroups Association, for example, is receiving grants totalling over £1 million in 1993/94 to support its programme of work with local playgroups, where children aged under 5 - mainly aged between 2½ and 4 - can be with their peers and learn through structured play opportunities. Over 700,000 children in this age group take part in playgroup sessions, which provide good preparation for compulsory schooling, as well as being enjoyable for the children and their parents, who are encouraged to take part. The National Association of Toy and Leisure

Libraries-also known as Play Matters-receives grant aid from the Department of Health to support its programme for support for local toy libraries. These help parents improve their parenting skills by offering opportunities to learn more about toys and how they can enhance children's development. The organisation also has a regular programme of assessment of new toys and publishes an annual Good Toy Guide.

Sport

7.59 The Government's sports policy statement, 'Sport and Active Recreation', published in 1991, identified the provision of opportunities for young people to take part in sport as a primary objective. The Department of National Heritage funds the Great Britain Sports Council which undertakes work in support of this objective. Several resource materials have been provided for primary school teachers, including "Teaching Children to Play Games". In March 1993, the Council published a policy document entitled, 'Young People and Sport: Policy and Frameworks for Action' and it is now considering a programme of follow-up action.

7.60 A high proportion of regional effort is devoted to ensuring that young people have the opportunity to realise their sporting potential and have access to the means to do so, in school and outside it, in community-based and club activities. A proportion of the grants which the Council gives to the governing bodies of sport and for the provision of new sports facilities benefits young people. The Council's regional offices also contribute funding to a national scheme called Champion Coaching, which is run by the National Coaching Foundation and provides quality after school coaching for 11-14 year olds. The Sports Council is undertaking a major piece of research on the extent of young people's participation in sport as a basis for further work in this area.

7.61 The Foundation for Sport and the Arts (FSA), which is funded partly by a reduction in Pool Betting Duty and partly by the football pools promoters, is grant-aiding a variety of sports projects for young people across the UK, as is the Government's new Business Sponsorship Incentive Scheme for the Sport, Sportmatch, which operates in England, Wales and Scotland.

7.62 The Sports Council for Wales, which is funded by the Welsh Office, has targeted £141,000 in 1993/94 specifically at children of school age. The Council's overall budget for local development services, which are aimed primarily at increasing sporting opportunities for young people, is £1.2m.

7.63 One of the main aims of the Scottish Sports Council is to increase sports participation for all the population in Scotland. Against a background of growing evidence of a serious decline in the number of schoolchildren participating in team games, the Scottish Sports Council, with specific funding from the Government, launched the TeamSport Scotland initiative in 1991. Under this scheme, TeamSport co-ordinators work closely with the sports governing bodies of the targeted sports to devise development programmes to stimulate the interest of youngsters in team sports. In addition to this work, the Scottish Sports Council is actively advising and assisting all governing bodies of sport to introduce structured youth development programmes.

7.64 The Sports Council for Northern Ireland is in the process of introducing a school-age sports strategy. This will seek to provide new sporting opportunities for young people throughout Northern Ireland. The strategy is directed at the District Councils, education and library boards and governing bodies of sport.

Arts and culture

7.65 The needs of children are also catered for in the field of arts and culture, through the activities of the Arts Council. The Arts Council's Dance Department encourages work in schools, for instance through its "Dance in Schools" initiative. The Arts Council has a dedicated fund for "Youth Arts", which in 1993/94 will receive £200,000, and which supports youth umbrella organisations covering dance, drama, music and opera. The Arts Council also has a very active Education Department which specialises in work to benefit young people. In addition the Arts Council has identified education as a priority for its work in 1994-95 and beyond.

7.66 The Regional Arts Boards also work to encourage cultural activity among children; the London Arts Board, for instance, offers advice and funding for training for the 33 Local Education Authorities and 2,500 schools in its area. Other examples include the training provided by the Northern Arts Board for artists to work with children, the funding provided by the East Midlands Arts Board for a Shakespeare in Schools project, the Eastern Arts Board which funds artists in schools in the visual arts, literature, music, drama and puppetry, and dance and mime.

7.67 One of the Welsh Arts Council's priorities is to encourage participation in the arts for all sections of the community, including children. It works with its partners to promote the value of arts in education, support arts activities in schools and community education, and encourage arts organisations to develop education activity. On dance, the Council has launched an Education Training initiative for dance professionals working in schools to deliver the dance element in the national Curriculum. The Council also operates a Theatre in Education programme which includes support for a national network of touring companies which visit schools and local theatres.

7.68 The Government is firmly committed to ensuring that children participate fully in cultural and artistic activities and that they have sufficient time for leisure. It seeks to achieve this through providing all children with a broad and balanced education; one which caters to their creative and recreational needs as well as to their academic needs. This is enshrined in law. The Education Reform Act 1988 (ERA) requires that all schools must have a curriculum which, among other things, promotes the spiritual, moral, cultural, mental and physical development of pupils at the school and of society.

7.69 The Government considers physical education, art and music to be an integral part of children's education and these subjects have therefore been identified as foundation subjects in the National Curriculum in England and Wales. The introduction of PE as a compulsory part of the curriculum for pupils aged 5-16 began in August 1992 and will be completed in August 1996. In Scotland, advice on physical education is contained in the document, 'National Guidelines. Expressive Arts 5-14'. This includes advice that physical education should provide all pupils with opportunities for the development of physical competencies, social skills, fitness and healthy lifestyles.

7.70 Although the organisation of the day is largely a matter for the governing body and head teacher of a school to decide, every day on which a school meets must be divided into two sessions separated by a break in the middle of the day (unless exceptional circumstances make this undesirable). This break allows children time for relaxation and affords them the opportunity to take part in leisure activities of their own, or of the school's, devising. The Scottish Office Education Department's 5-14 Programme guidelines contain similar provisions to those in the National Curriculum in England and Wales for leisure, recreation and cultural activities.

Environmental Activities

7.71 Research carried out for the Department of the Environment has shown that young people are keen to be involved in environmental action, particularly in their own local area. The Department of the Environment launched the "Green Brigade" initiative to encourage young people to direct their environmental energy towards practical action. At an environmental summit in Manchester in September 1993 participants discussed their environmental concerns and selected nine projects to receive funding under the initiative. The projects are located in different parts of the country and all involve local children, schools and youth groups. The Green Brigade has also produced two activity packs for children, on litter and recycling and on energy efficiency. Green Brigade Week will be held in March 1994.

Chapter 8: Special Protection measures

Refugee children - Article 22

8.1   The comprehensive provision in UK law for the care and protection of children applies in full to children who have been recognised as refugees in this country and to those who have sought asylum here, but whose claim has not been determined. The UK has entered a reservation on immigration but this does not inhibit the discharge of our obligations under Article 22. The UK is, of course, party to the 1951 UN Convention Relating to the Status of Refugees, and honours its obligations under this Convention in full.

8.2   Domestic legislation governing the handling of asylum applications is the Asylum and Immigration Appeals Act 1993. Because the issues raised in determining whether an individual is or is not a refugee within the meaning of the 1951 Convention are the same whether the applicant is an adult or a child the Act itself makes no distinction between adult and child asylum seekers other than to build in safeguards (at Section 3(2)) in respect of the fingerprinting of children under the age of 16.

8.3   The Immigration Rules (which are a statement by the Home Secretary of the practice to be followed in the exercise of his general powers to regulate the entry into and stay of persons in the UK) do, however, now contain specific reference to children. Paragraph 180(O) allows for any child accompanying an asylum applicant as a dependant to be granted leave to enter or remain on the same terms as the principal applicant if any such leave is granted once the asylum application has been resolved; and makes clear that children will not normally be interviewed in such circumstances unless this is necessary to establish a particular child's identity.   These provisions are intended to minimise the exposure of a child to the bureaucratic procedures which are an inevitable feature of the asylum determination process.

8.4   Unaccompanied children are also mentioned in the Rules.   The purpose of Paragraphs 190P - 180R is to highlight the peculiar vulnerability of lone child asylum seekers; and to lay down certain guidelines for the conduct of interviews in such cases and for the interpretation of what a child might say in support of his/her claim. The emphasis is very heavily on the welfare of the child. We recognise that any interview can be a difficult experience for a child, even when accompanied by an adult he or she trusts, and the Rules make it quite plain that a child should only be interviewed if it is absolutely unavoidable. The terms of these additions to the Rules were discussed and agreed before publication with a wide range of interested parties including Non-Governmental Organisations (NGOs) such as the (British) Refugee Council and the Children's Legal Centre.   Their presence can be taken as a statement of the UK's intent fully to discharge its obligations under Article 22.

8.5   The UK recognises the need to reach quick decisions on asylum applications from unaccompanied children and gives such applications priority. In addition, the Home Office has embarked, with the Refugee Council and the Children's Legal Centre, on the development of a comprehensive training programme for a limited number of its staff who will specialise in interviewing child asylum seekers. Issues likely to be addressed in the training programme include:

i   adult/child communication (establishing a rapport)

ii   promoting feelings of trust and security

iii   overcoming a child's inhibitions

iv   "reading the signs" when a child is unable to express himself verbally

v   pace of questioning

vi   understanding the cultural background and ensuring that any interpreter used is appropriate in terms of sex, ethnic origin, dialect etc.

vii   ensuring the child's physical comfort (eg watching for signs of tiredness and distress, providing toilet facilities etc).

8.6   We hope that training will have begun by the end of 1993. Once completed it is intended that all interviews involving child asylum seekers (including those currently conducted by Immigration Officers at the ports) will be undertaken by these specially trained staff.

8.7   A further measure of the UK's determination to safeguard child asylum seekers is its decision to fund the establishment of a non-statutory Panel of Advisers for unaccompanied children. Co-ordinated by the Refugee Council, this Panel will provide unaccompanied children with an individual adviser/friend who will help them in their dealings with the various agencies with an interest in their situation (eg Home Office, local authority Social Service Departments, Benefits Agency etc). So far as possible, this will be someone from a similar ethnic background as the child, and they will clearly need an understanding of the functions of the various agencies with which the child will have to deal as its case progresses. The adviser will be entirely independent of any arm of the UK Government and should be in a position to gain the trust of the child concerned. It is not expected that he/she will provide the child with legal advice on the handling of the asylum claim; there are already publicly funded bodies in the UK which have this responsibility, and child asylum seekers are eligible for legal aid.

8.8   It is also worth mentioning that special arrangements to cater for the welfare of unaccompanied children have been made with the Social Services Department of Croydon Borough Council. The Immigration and Nationality Department Public Enquiry Office is based in Croydon, and unaccompanied children sometimes arrive here to claim asylum. Our close liaison with the Council assures that children arriving at our offices in these circumstances can be taken into care quickly and without fuss. Similar arrangements are in place or about to be introduced with local authorities in the vicinity of our major air and sea ports.

8.9   The principle of family reunion is fully recognised in the UK, and as with any adult, a child recognised as a refugee within the meaning of the 1951 Convention is generally entitled to seek immediate reunion with close family members. Our general policy on those granted Exceptional Leave to Remain (ELR) (ie those who have not been recognised as a refugee as defined in the 1951 Convention but who, for humanitarian or practical reasons, we have decided should not be required to return to their country of origin) is that they should wait until they have been in the country with that status for 4 years before bringing other members of their family here. This is because ELR is, in the first instance, a temporary status, often granted for reasons not directly connected with the basis of the original asylum claim. It is right in our view that sufficient time should have elapsed for us to establish whether that status is likely to become permanent before the question of family reunion is addressed.

8.10   Having said this, there is discretion to depart from this rule if the circumstances of a particular case warrant such action, and the very fact that a child is unaccompanied is often enough to trigger the exercise of this discretion.   This would mean that if one or both parents of an unaccompanied child (or, in the absence of the parents, siblings) could be found we would certainly consider the options for reuniting the child with his family. In the case of those recognised as Convention refugees this is likely to mean that the family members will be allowed to come here on the grounds that reunion in the country of origin is not possible (although if the relatives concerned have found refuge in another safe country themselves it might be more appropriate for the child to join them there - this would depend very much on the circumstances of the individual case, and we would always take advice from UNHCR on the most suitable option).

8.11   A similar outcome is quite possible in the case of a child who has ELR, although in these cases we reserve the right to pursue the option of returning the child to family members in his own country (if any such have been identified) so long as we, UNHCR and other agencies with responsibility for the welfare of the child are satisfied that there will be adequate arrangements for his long term care and well being. Such cases are the exception rather than the rule but we do not accept that the presence in this country of an unaccompanied child gives close relatives an <u>automatic</u> right to come here too, or that this will necessarily always be in the best interests of the child; it can in some circumstances be better for the child to rejoin his family in his own country.

8.12   The UK is always willing to help the United Nations High Commission for Refugees or any other competent organisation with measures they may have in hand to identify the relatives of an unaccompanied child refugee or asylum seekers.

8.13   This summary of the UK's approach to child asylum seekers illustrates that we have done much to put our approach to such cases on a systematic basis, and we are generally satisfied that we are adhering to our obligations under Article 22.   Children seeking asylum are not in general detained; their cases are given priority; and there is an extensive network of provisions now in place to ensure that the child:

> i   has every opportunity to present his claim in calm and non-threatening circumstances, at his own pace, in his own language, and with ready access to independent advice; and
>
> ii   is given a secure and comfortable environment in which to live and develop both while the asylum claim is outstanding and afterwards for so long as he remains in the UK. The secure and comfortable environment includes having the same access to the National Health Service as every other UK child. The Department of Health is currently arranging for the Refugee Council to be provided with a list of child mental health professionals willing to be contacted where there is concern for the mental health of a refugee child or adolescent.

Education and Article 22

8.14   The Education Act 1944, as amended by the Education Act 1980, places local education authorities (LEAs) in England and Wales under a duty to make education available for all school-age children in their area, appropriate to their age, abilities and aptitudes.   This duty extends to all children residing in their area, whether permanently or temporarily and includes the children of displaced persons.

8.15   The Government provides funding to meet the basic educational needs of displaced persons in the same way and at the same rate as for other pupils.   In addition, the Government provides grants payable under Section 210 of the Education Reform Act 1988 for additional educational provision for those who are for the time being resident in a camp or other accommodation or establishment provided exclusively for refugees or for displaced or similar persons.

8.16 The Local Government (Amendment) Act 1993 amended section 11 of the Local Government Act 1966 so as to remove its restriction to those of Commonwealth origin. This should make matters easier for schools which have both Commonwealth and non-Commonwealth pupils on roll and for those where the pupils are predominantly from non-Commonwealth countries. It will provide LEAs with the opportunity to adjust their priorities and rationalise provision, in the light of local needs and circumstances.

Children in Armed Conflicts - Article 38, including physical and psychological recovery and social reintegration - Article 39

8.17 The UK is a party to the Fourth Geneva Convention relative to the Protection of Civilian Persons in Time of War. This emphasises that women and children shall be the object of special respect and shall be protected against any form of assault. It also provides for the reunion of dispersed families, wherever possible. Above all, it entitles every person affected by armed conflict to his fundamental rights and guarantees without discrimination. The UK is also a party to the Convention relating to the Status of Stateless Persons, and the Convention and the Protocol relating to the status of refugees. At CHR49, the UK supported a resolution (1993/83) on the Consequences of Armed Conflicts on Children's Lives. This noted the need to implement effective protection for children against the adverse consequences of armed conflicts.

8.18 The UK's policies on the minimum age of recruits to the armed forces and the participation of under 18 year olds in armed conflict are in accordance with the provisions of international law, namely Article 77 of the First Additional Protocol to the Geneva Conventions 1949. The minimum age for recruitment to the British Armed Forces is 16. In the Royal Navy, no under 17s are drafted to submarines, and no under 18s are employed as aircrew in any of the Services. In addition, the following minimum ages apply to emergency service overseas and in Northern Ireland:

	Minimum age for Service Overseas	Minimum age for Service in N Ireland
Royal Navy	18 if shore based 16 for surface ships	18
Royal Marines	18 if shore based 17 for operational tours	18
Army	17 1/4	18 for service "on the streets" 17 1/2 if restricted to barracks
Royal Air Force	17 1/2	18

8.19 For under 18s the age of the recruit is taken into account in determining the type of duties they are employed on. Under 18s are less likely to take part in hostilities than over 18s and they require their parents' or guardians' written consent to enlist.

The administration of juvenile justice - Article 40

8.20 Section 44(1) of the Children and Young Persons Act 1933 states that every court in dealing with a child or young person who is brought before it, either as an offender or otherwise, shall have regard to the proper welfare of the child or young person and shall take steps for ensuring his removal from undesirable surroundings and for securing proper care provision is made for education and training.

8.21 It is a general principle that a statute on criminal offences, normally only affects factual situations which arise during the period of its operation. This applies equally to both adults and children.

8.22 It is a fundamental principle of our criminal justice system that a person is innocent until proven guilty. This applies equally to both children and adults.

8.23 All juveniles charged with an offence are taken to court. They are usually dealt with by a special magistrates court known as a youth court or for more serious offences in the adult court system. Courts are normally required to order the parents of children under the age of 16 to attend with their children (section 34 of the Children and young Persons Act 1933 (as amended) applies). For 16 and 17 year olds the court has a power rather than a duty to order the parents to attend. This requirement can be varied where the court considers it would not be appropriate for the parent to attend (ie if the parent is the victim). As for adults children have a right to legal representation and for those who cannot afford it, financial assistance is available under the Legal Aid Act 1988.

The right to silence

8.24   The Government is introducing a bill into Parliament which will allow, in certain circumstances, a court to draw proper inferences from an accused's failure or refusal to answer questions. Children under the age of 14 are exempted from the proposed legislation.

8.25   A defendant has an automatic right of appeal to the Crown Court following conviction at a Youth or Magistrates' Court. However, leave to appeal to the Court of Appeal, on a Crown Court decision, must be sought and may be granted by a single judge under section 31(1) of the Criminal Appeal Act 1968. Depending on the court in which the case was first heard, and the nature of the appeal, further appeal lies to the High Court or the Court of Appeal. Finally appeal lies to the House of Lords, but only where it has been certified that a point of law of general public importance is involved and that the court or the House of Lords has given leave to appeal.

8.26   The Government recognises the right of all persons involved in Court proceedings to be able to understand what is taking place. The provision of interpreters is organised by the Lord Chancellor's Department.

8.27   No newspaper may reveal the name and address, school or any other identifying particulars of a child brought before a youth court (by virtue of section 49 of the Children and Young Persons Act 1933) and in the case of a child tried in the adult court system the court has a power to direct the above where children are concerned.

8.28   The position in England and Wales is that a child under the age of 10 is incapable, in law, of committing a criminal offence and may not be dealt with under the criminal law. The full position on ages of criminal liability in England, Wales, Scotland and Northern Ireland was set out in Chapter 2 of the report.

8.29 In recent years Government policy on young offenders has concentrated on diverting young people away from crime and discouraging imprisonment and criminalisation of those young people who are arrested and charged with an offence. The focus has been on cautioning and community sentencing. During the 1980s there was a substantial decline in the use of custody for juveniles. The Intermediate Treatment Initiative was launched in January 1983, involving the development of intensive community based schemes which could act as alternatives to care orders and custodial disposals for juvenile offenders. The Initiative was generally regarded as being highly successful, and re-offending rates were found to be significantly lower in Initiative areas.

8.30   It is recognised both in theory and in practice that the delay in entry of a young person into the formal justice system may help prevent his entry into the system altogether. This is reflected in the fact that the majority of children who admit their offence are cautioned for the offence rather than brought to court. This is set out in Home Office guidance on cautioning. Where a decision is taken not to caution a child, the Crown Prosecution Service Codes state that a prosecution should only be continued with if the spirit of the cautioning advice has been applied.

8.31   The law requires that all courts dealing with children should have regard to their welfare . A wide range of non-custodial orders is available for sentencing children and young people. These are high quality community schemes which conform to national standards, including attendance centre orders, supervision orders, community service orders, combination orders and probation orders. Under the Criminal Justice Act 1991, courts' powers to make these orders are restricted in cases which are serious enough to warrant such a sentence. Any community sentence must be one that is suitable to the offender and the restrictions on the liberty of the offender imposed by the order must be commensurate with the seriousness of the offence.

8.32   The legal system in Northern Ireland complies with the terms of this Article.   Children under 10 years of age are presumed not to have the capacity to infringe the penal law.

Children deprived of their liberty, including any form of detention, imprisonment or placement in custodial settings - Article 37 b, c and d.

The Children Act

8.33   Under powers in the Children Act 1989 no child may have his liberty restricted unless statutory criteria apply. The maximum period a child may have their liberty restricted without the authority of the Court is 72 hours. The child has the right to be legally represented when such applications are considered, and is eligible to apply for legal aid for such purposes, and to appeal against any such decision of the Court.

8.34   No child under the age of 13 may have his liberty restricted in secure accommodation in a Community Home without the prior approval of the

Secretary of State to the placement.

8.35 Provision is made for the case of every child in secure accommodation in a Community Home to be reviewed (both as to the continued application of the statutory criteria and the need to keep him in such accommodation) within one month of the inception of the placement and not less frequently than every three months while the placement continues.

8.36 Further change to those arrangements introduced in October 1992 have been made to introduce an independent element amongst those appointed to undertake the review of such placements, and to ensure that the child, his parents or others with parental responsibility are notified of the outcome of those reviews and the local authority's reasons for taking, or not taking, such action.

8.37 The statutory safeguards relating to restriction of liberty of children looked after by local authorities in the Children Act have been extended, by Regulation, to apply to children placed by health and education authorities. However, such latter authorities are not legally bound to apply various aspects of the arrangements (approval of accommodation; placement of children under 13; review of placement, and the keeping of records).

Arrest and detention

8.38 The powers of the police to arrest and detain persons, including children, are defined by the Police and Criminal Evidence Act 1984 (PACE). PACE describes the circumstances in which a person may be arrested and the period of time for which he or she may subsequently be detained at a police station without charge. A child may only be detained for up to 24 hours without charge or 36 hours in the case of a serious arrestable offence upon the authority of a senior officer and on the authority of a magistrate for up to a total not exceeding 96 hours. At the expiry of the period the police must either charge the child and bring him before a magistrates court as soon as possible or release him with charge either on bail or without bail.

8.39 PACE and its accompanying codes of practice make special provision for juveniles in police custody. When a child or young person is arrested the appropriate adult must be informed. This means his or her parent or guardian or, if the child is in care, the local authority or voluntary organisation he or she is with. Failing the parent or guardian, notification should be made to a social worker or to another responsible adult who is not a police officer.

8.40 The custody officer should as soon as practicable inform the adult of the grounds for the child or young person's detention and his or her whereabouts; and should ask the adult to come to the police station. It is the function of the appropriate adult to advise and assist the child, and the child may consult privately with him or her at any time.

8.41 A juvenile must not be interviewed or asked to provide or sign a written statement in the absence of the appropriate adult, except in narrowly defined circumstances. A juvenile should not be placed in police cells unless no other secure accommodation is available or the custody officer considers that it is not practicable to supervise him or her if he or she is not in a cell with an adult.

8.42 An intimate search of a juvenile (that is, one involving the examination of body orifices) may only take place in the presence of an appropriate adult of the same sex, subject to the wishes of the juvenile.

8.43 Every child has the right to legal advice and assistance. The Codes of Practice for Detention and Treatment and Questioning of Persons by Police provide that an arrested person (adult or child) has a right to consult privately with a solicitor and to be advised that independent legal advice is available free of charge. A child has the right to challenge the legality of his detention through the courts. Where a court decides there is no legal justification for a person being held, a writ of habeas corpus can be issued against the person who is enforcing the detention.

Arrest and Detention - Scotland

8.44 If a child is arrested on suspicion of a criminal offence he/she is taken to a police station and the circumstances reviewed by an officer of the rank of inspector or the officer in charge. Under section 3 of the Criminal Justice (Scotland) Act 1980 a parent or guardian must be informed of where the child is being detained as soon as possible. The child will normally be released into the care of the parent or guardian unless;

i   the crime/offence is grave; or

ii   it is necessary to remove him or her from bad associations; or

iii   release would defeat the ends of justice.

8.45 If the child is not released as above he/she must be detained in a "place of safety" other than a police station for example a children's home until he/she can be brought before a sheriff. Under the provisions of the Social Work (Scotland) Act 1968 a child can only be detained in a police station when:

i   it is impractical to detain him/her elsewhere; or

ii   the child is so unruly that he/she cannot be safely detained elsewhere; or

iii   it is necessary by reason of the child's physical or mental health.

If such action is considered necessary the officer in charge of the station must prepare a certificate specifying the reason for doing so.

8.46 When a child commits a criminal offence and is arrested he/she is interviewed, cautioned and charged by the police in the presence of a parent or guardian. A full report is then submitted through the local Community Involvement branch to either the Reporter to the Children's Panel or the Procurator Fiscal.

8.47 Police powers of search are the same for a child as for an adult but normally a responsible person for example parent or guardian will be present.

Imprisonment

8.48 There are no sentences of imprisonment for children, however children can be sentenced to a period of detention in a young offender institution. A court can only pass a custodial sentence (in the case of both young offenders and adults) where certain criteria are met. These are that the offence or the combination of the offence and one or more offences associated with it, are so serious that only a custodial sentence can be justified for the offence or, where the offence is a violent or sexual offence, only such a sentence would be adequate to protect the public.

8.49 Custodial sentences, other than those for grave crimes, are not available until the age of 15 and for a maximum period of 12 months (by virtue of section 1 of the Criminal Justice Act 1988). There are plans to increase the maximum period to two years. There are also plans to introduce a new sentence of detention, a Secure Training Order, for children aged 12-14 who persistently offend and who have not responded to supervision in the community and who meet the criteria for custodial sentences set out above. The proposed sentence maximum sentence is for two years. The sentence will be different from anything tried before. The emphasis will not be on punishment but on providing children with the skills they need to give up their offending behaviour through an intensive supervision to ensure their successful re-introduction into society. If the measure gains parliamentary approval, it is likely to be introduced within the next two years.

8.50 For grave crimes, that is those which in the case of an adult could carry a maximum sentence of imprisonment of 14 years or more, long terms of detention are available from the age of 14 and the age of 10 for murder and manslaughter by virtue of section 53 of the Children and Young Persons Act 1933. In addition, a section 53 sentence is available for 14-17 year olds who are convicted of offences of causing death by dangerous driving or causing death by careless driving while under the influence of drink or drugs for which the maximum penalty for an adult is ten years. In the case of 16 and 17 year olds, a section 53 sentence is also available for the offence of indecent assault on a woman. There are plans to extend the scope of section 53 detention so that it applies to all children from the age of 10 who have been convicted of a grave crime which carries a sentence of 14 years or more or in the case of the offence of indecent assault on a woman.

8.51   In Scotland, children who have not yet attained 16, convicted on indictment, may be sentenced to be detained for a specified period. Children cannot be imprisoned, and custodial sentences are used only where the court is of the opinion that there is no other method of dealing with the child. During that period, the child is liable to be detained in such a place and on such conditions as the Secretary of State may direct under the Criminal Procedure (Scotland) Act 1975.

8.52   Where a person under 18 is convicted of murder he must be sentenced to be detained without limit of time. He may be detained in a place, and under such conditions as directed by the Secretary of State.

8.53   Children appearing in sheriff courts in summary proceedings may, if convicted, be detained in residential care by the appropriate local authority for a period not exceeding one year. A child may only be sentenced to be detained if he is found guilty of an offence in respect of which it is competent to impose imprisonment on a person aged 27 or more.

8.54   In Northern Ireland the spirit of Article 37(b) is met by current legislation such as the Police and Criminal Evidence Order. As regards Article 37(c) it is the policy of the criminal justice system in Northern Ireland to maintain separation, where possible, between children and adults.

8.55   The UK entered a reservation to the effect that where at any time there is a lack of suitable accommodation or adequate facilities for a particular individual in any institution in which young offenders are detained, or where the mixing of adults and children is deemed to be mutually beneficial, (such as in the case of women and young girls) we reserved the right not to apply Article 37(c) in so far as those provisions require children who are detained to be accommodated separately from adults.

Number of children in secure accommodation on 31 March 1992, by legal status on admission, sex and age

| | Age on Admission | | | | | | | | | | | | | |
| | 11 | | 12 | | 13 | | 14 | | 15 | | 16 | | 17 | |
	M	F	M	F	M	F	M	F	M	F	M	F	M	F
England	1	-	5	3	17	6	31	13	65	19	61	13	2	2
Detained - S53 Children and Young Persons Act 1933	-	1	1	-	-	-	13	2	27	3	33	1	1	-
Others	1	-	4	3	17	6	18	11	38	16	28	12	1	2

The sentencing of juveniles, in particular the prohibition of capital punishment and life imprisonment - Article 37 a

8.56   There is no death penalty for children in the United Kingdom.

8.57   Under the Children and Young Persons Act of 1933, anyone found guilty of murder under the age of 18 at the time of the offence is sentenced to detention during Her Majesty's Pleasure, not to life imprisonment. Detention may be in a local authority home, a Youth Training Centre, special hospital, youth custody centre, Young Offenders Institution, or if detained long enough, an ordinary prison.

8.58   A person convicted of an offence other than murder for which a life sentence may be passed on an adult may be sentenced to detention for life under the Children and Young Persons Act 1933. This sentence has the same effect as one of detention during Her Majesty's Pleasure.

8.59   A person under 21 convicted of murder is sentenced to "custody for life" unless liable to be detained during Her Majesty's Pleasure.

8.60   A person aged 17 or over convicted of an offence for which a life sentence may be passed on an adult may be sentenced to "custody for life".

8.61   Custody for life is similar to a life sentence except that the Secretary of State may from time to time direct that an offender who is female, or who is male and under 22 years of age, is to be detained in a youth custody centre instead of a prison.

8.62   Detainees <u>may</u> be released on licence, subject to conditions, on the recommendation of a Parole Board. The date of release will depend on the circumstances of the case and the views of the Lord Chief Justice and trial judge (if available).

8.63 The Children and Young Persons Act (Northern Ireland) 1968 provides that neither capital punishment nor life imprisonment without the possibility of release shall be imposed for offences committed by persons under 18 years of age.

Physical and psychological recovery and social reintegration of children - Article 39

8.64 The Department of Health launched a centrally funded child abuse treatment initiative in 1990/91. The first stage of the initiative was the National Children's Home survey of existing treatment facilities for abused children and young perpetrators. The Department of Health is currently making grants to support a number of projects by voluntary organisations providing different types and ranges of treatment. The total made available over the five year period since the inception of the initiative will be £1.8 million.

8.65 Many of the more severely abused children will require to be treated by the NHS. Every child suspected of having been sexually abused will need to be assessed under the child protection procedures set out in the government's guidance Working Together. Not all these cases will be proven. Of those who are, all will need protection, but not all will show emotional disturbance significant enough to require additional specialist therapeutic intervention.

Economic exploitation, including child labour - Article 32

Definition of the Child

8.66 Because the Convention defines as a child a person below 18 years of age, the UK felt it necessary to enter a reservation relating to this Article. This is because, in common with adult workers, those aged above the minimum school leaving age (around the child's 16th birthday - see remarks on Article 1) are generally free to negotiate their hours and other conditions of employment with the employer.

Health and Safety

8.67 The UK has a comprehensive system to protect the interests of children at work. Briefly, no child may work in industrial undertakings or undertake any work that is likely to be harmful to his physical health or likely to affect his education. Generally, no child under the age of 13 may work. In addition no child may work before 7.00am and after 7.00pm; work for more than 2 hours on any school day or Sunday; work for more than 5 hours on a Saturday or school holiday if they are under 15, those over 15 are restricted to 8 hours on such days. Children may not work during the school holidays for more than 25 hours a week if under 15 or more than 35 hours a week if over 15.

8.68   Most health and safety legislation is not age specific and Health and Safety Executive and local authority inspectors enforce it irrespective of the age of the employee.   There are some substances, machines or processes (examples are lead, ionising radiation, woodworking machines) which pose a specific risk to the health and safety of young people.   In these cases regulations generally prevent young people under 18 from doing the activity.

8.69   Section 2 of the Health and Safety at Work Act lays a duty on employers "to conduct their undertaking in such a way as to ensure, so far as reasonably practicable, the health, safety and welfare at work of all his employees".   In addition, the Health and Safety (Training for Employment) Regulations 1990 mean that employers are required to treat trainees on work experience as employees.   Under the Management of Health and Safety at Work Regulations 1992, employers are required to assess the risks in their workplace and they would need to take into account the fact that in general children are smaller, weaker and less mature and responsible than adults and may need greater supervision and more extensive training. Employers must ensure that their specific needs are met and that they are not drawn into work activities inappropriate to their state of health or any disability.

Drug misuse - Article 33

General

8.70   The UK Government has drawn up a comprehensive strategy to protect all its citizens, including children, from the dangers of drug misuse. This strategy recognises that the different aspects of the problem are inter-related and that it is necessary to tackle both the supply of, and demand for, drugs.   The aim is to reduce the supply of drugs by:

i   supporting international efforts to curb the production and trafficking of drugs

ii   strengthening Customs and police enforcement

iii   ensuring the controls on licit drugs produced and prescribed in this country are adequate to prevent diversion to the illicit market

iv   deterring drug traffickers and dealers by high maximum penalties and by high maximum penalties and by depriving them of the proceeds of their crimes.

Demand for drugs is being tackled by:

i   discouraging those who not misusing drugs from doing so

ii   helping those who are already misusing to stop.

Prevention

8.71 The government also promotes national anti-drugs and anti-solvents publicity campaigns which aim to inform the various target groups of the dangers of becoming involved with drug misuse. While the focus of earlier campaigns was primarily young people in the 13-20 age group, current phases of the campaign are aimed at raising parental awareness of the problems of drug and solvent misuse among young people. European Drug Prevention Week held in November 1992 focused on young people aged 8-21 and aimed to raise awareness of the dangers of drug and solvent misuse. The UK will be participating in a second European Drug Prevention Week in October 1994, which will again have the theme of drug prevention and the young. Other UK initiatives include two competitions for schools to encourage young people to think about substance misuse issues, and the production of various information leaflets for young people.

8.72 The Home Office Drugs Prevention Initiative was launched in October 1989. Its aim is to respond quickly and effectively to concerns within the local community, and to stimulate, encourage and support ideas of work to prevent the spread of drugs misuse, particularly among young people, including those of school age.

8.73 Under the Initiative 20 local drugs prevention teams have been set up in those areas of Great Britain where there is considered to be a substantial risk from the threat of drugs misuse. The teams, which are managed and supported by a Central Drugs Prevention Unit within the Home Office, work closely with a wide range of statutory and voluntary agencies, including the local authorities, schools, police, and probation services and specialist agencies. They are also drawing in parents, youth organisations and any other bodies who have a keen interest or valuable role in stemming the numbers of young people and others who become involved in drugs.

8.74 Each team has funds available to support local drugs prevention projects. The Central Drugs Prevention Unit is stimulating and reinforcing drugs prevention activity in those areas of the country where local drug prevention teams do not operate and has a small central grants fund available for that purpose. To date over 250 projects worth in excess of £1.1 million have been targeted at young people specifically. These have included publicity and information campaigns, peer education projects, diversionary activities and training programmes for youth workers.

Drugs Education

8.75 The UK Government recognises that the education service has an important part to play in the overall strategy to combat drugs misuse. Government policy in this area is to stimulate, encourage and support work within schools and the youth service with a view to ensuring that young people are made aware of the dangers of drug misuse, and are equipped with the knowledge, skills and attitudes they will need to make well informed, independent judgements to resist negative peer and other pressures, and to safeguard their long term good health.

8.76 Under the provisions of the Education Reform Act 1988, all maintained schools in England and Wales are now required to provide education about drugs as part of National Curriculum science. In addition, the National Curriculum Council, set up under the provisions of that Act, has issued guidance to schools on the place and content of health education, including substance use and misuse, in the wider curriculum.

8.77 In Scotland the curriculum in Scottish schools is not prescribed by statute. The responsibility for the delivery and content of the curriculum rests with education authorities and head teachers. However national guidance is issued by the Scottish Office Education Department and the Scottish Consultative Council on the Curriculum. In April 1993 new guidelines were published on teaching environmental studies to 5-14 year olds. These give health education a firm place in the curriculum and highlight drugs education as a key feature.

8.78 The UK Government has taken a range of other initiatives in recent years, for example, providing funds both for the development of curriculum materials for use in primary schools, secondary schools and the youth service, and for voluntary organisations to develop health-related educational initiatives. As a result, schools are now in a much stronger position than ever before to provide effective health education.

Treatment and Rehabilitation

8.79 Government guidelines state that every District Health Authority should have access to the following range of services

i   advice and counselling

ii   in-patient and community de-toxification facilities

iii   residential rehabilitation

iv   follow-up support where needed

8.80   The voluntary sector plays a leading role in counselling and residential rehabilitation establishments. Statutory health care authorities normally provide de-toxification facilities on a regional basis or take place on an out-patient basis under expert medical supervision.

8.81   The range of workers providing services across both the statutory and voluntary sectors includes doctors, community psychiatric nurses, social workers, youth workers and specialist drug workers. The Government also encourages General Practitioners to become involved with service provision for drug misusers.

Action on illegal Drugs importation

8.82   The start of the Single Market on 1 January 1993 required the opening of borders to permit the free flow of traffic both passenger and commercial between EC countries. HM Customs and Excise right to stop and search all persons or freight entering the UK became limited to that from 3rd (non-EC) countries. Article 36 of the Treaty of Rome, however, permits members to maintain border controls to protect society from such social evils as the effects of drugs, pornography and organised crime. Under this article, to allow the continued detection of drugs and pornography at border controls Customs developed "Light Touch" controls. These are intelligence based and targeted at those areas where the risk of such importations is perceived to be highest. One way in which the Department of Customs and Excise has developed its intelligence network has been the implementation of the Anti-Drugs Alliance. The Alliance was developed from the Customs Cooperation Councils initiative of Memorandum of Understanding. The initiative aimed primarily at the Transport industry is entirely voluntary and enables Customs to gain access to trade computer systems and for trade members to act as Customs' "eyes and ears" while doing their normal jobs.

Sexual exploitation and sexual abuse - Article 34

8.83   The Government takes the view that the sexual abuse of children is totally unacceptable wherever, or by whomsoever, it is committed. This is reflected in our own law, which is particularly severe in relation to sexual offences against children. As well as the information given under this Article, our contribution on Article 19 earlier in the report sets out in detail the action being taken to combat the problem of child abuse.

8.84 There are various statutes which relate to sexual offences against children. Details of these with the maximum penalties are set out below:

Section	Offences	Maximum penalty
Sexual Offences Act 1956		
s.1	Rape	Life
s.5	Intercourse with a girl under 13	Life
s.6	Intercourse with a girl under 16	2 years
s.10	Incest by a man	If victim under 13 life, otherwise 7 years
s.11	Incest by a woman	7 years
s.12	Buggery	Life
s.14	Indecent assault on a woman	10 years
s.15	Indecent assault on a man	10 years
s.16	Assault with intent to commit buggery	2 years
s.19	Abduction of girl under 18 from parent or guardian	2 years
s.20	Abduction of girl under 16 from parent or guardian	2 years
s.22	Causing prostitution of a woman anywhere in the world	2 years
s.23	Procuration of a girl under 21 to have unlawful sexual intercourse in any part of the world	2 years
s.25	Permitting a girl under 13 to use premises for intercourse	Life
s.26	Permitting a girl under 16 to use premises for intercourse	2 years
s.28	Causing or encouraging prostitution etc of girl under 16	2 years
s.32	Solicitation by a man	2 years
Indecency with children Act 1960		
s.1	Indecency with a child	2 years

continued...

Section	Offences	Maximum Penalty
Sexual Offences Act 1967		
s.5	Living on the earnings of male prostitution	7 years
Criminal Law Act 1977		
s.54	Incitement to commit incest	2 years
Protection of Children Act 1978		
s.1	Taking or permitting to be taken indecent photographs of children (includes films or videos)	3 years
Criminal Justice Act 1988		
s.160	Possession of indecent photographs of children	£5,000 fine

The table below gives the number of persons convicted of the main sexual offences against children in England and Wales from 1987

	1987	1988	1989	1990	1991
Buggery with a boy under the age of 16 or with a woman or an animal	195	232	183	189	168
Attempt to commit buggery with a boy under the age of 16 or a woman or an animal	20	31	26	18	26
Indecent assault on a male under 16 years	430	460	406	421	351
Indecent assault on a female aged under 16	1,556	1,650	1,657	1,537	1,469
Unlawful sexual intercourse with a girl aged under 13 years	102	135	96	110	105
Unlawful sexual intercourse with a girl aged under 16 years	346	340	262	304	223
Incest with a girl under 13 years	89	104	100	84	68
Inciting girl under 16 years to have incestuous sexual intercourse	4	2	5	3	3
Householder permitting unlawful sexual intercourse with a girl under 16	6	7	3	5	1
Person responsible for girl aged under 16 causing or encouraging her prostitution etc	3	1	1	2	2
Abduction of unmarried girl aged under 16 years	7	8	13	8	8
Gross indecency with children	248	246	219	276	219

Sexual Offences committed abroad

8.85   It has been suggested that, in order to fulfil our obligation under the terms of Article 34, the jurisdiction of our courts should be extended, to enable them to prosecute British citizens who are alleged to have committed sexual offences against children while abroad. The Government does not accept this view. Any attempt to prosecute British citizens in the United Kingdom for offences committed abroad would encounter considerable difficulties of both practice and principle. Our police have no power to gather evidence or to enforce the law in foreign countries, our courts would be unable to compel the attendance of foreign witnesses. Our prosecuting authorities would be unable to prepare a sufficiently strong case for them successfully to prosecute someone suspected of committing offences abroad.

8.86   There might also be particular difficulties in cases involving alleged sexual offences against minors, because different societies have widely differing law about the age at which a child can consent to sexual relations. For example, in many EC cases the age of consent may be as young as 12. We do not believe it would be appropriate to prosecute someone in this country for behaviour which was lawful in the place where it occurred, any more than it would be appropriate for a foreign state to prosecute someone for lawful activities carried out in this country.

8.87   However, if a British citizen has broken the law of a foreign country, by abusing children while visiting, the UK government do not believe that it is acceptable for them to avoid prosecution when they return to this country. Some countries take a wide jurisdiction over the activities of their nationals abroad, but this reflects the fact that they are constitutionally prohibited from extraditing their own nationals. Unlike them, we are willing to extradite British nationals to stand trial in the places where their alleged offences were committed, and we take the view that it is the prerogative of a sovereign state to enforce the law on its own territory. The United Kingdom has an extradition treaty with Thailand where there are, as the Committee will be aware, particular problems with child prostitution, and those UK citizens who abuse children in Thailand therefore face the prospect of being returned to stand trial there, provided the Thai authorities request this.

8.88   In addition, the Government passed the Criminal Justice (International Co-operation) Act 1990 in order to enable us to assist criminal investigations in foreign countries. This may include arranging for the service of summonses and other legal documents in this country, arranging for statements to be taken from witnesses here, arranging for a person in custody to travel abroad to assist in proceedings, and in certain cases arranging for the search of premises here and the seizure of documents or other evidence.

8.89   Of course, the United Kingdom can only help to deal in this way with a case involving child prostitution in another country when we receive a request from the appropriate authorities. There is a limit to what we can do in helping to enforce the law in a foreign state, and the main responsibility for dealing with the problem of child exploitation overseas will necessarily remain with the authorities of the state concerned.

8.90   This does not mean to say that the United Kingdom has been, or intends to be, complacent, and we have raised this issue at an international level.   At the 1993 session of the Commission on Human Rights, we co-sponsored a resolution implementing a programme of action for the prevention of the sale of children, child prostitution, and child pornography.   At the United Nations General Assembly in 1992, we introduced a resolution on the problem of street children.   It was adopted by consensus, and we are following up both resolutions at the Commission on Human Rights in 1994.

8.91   In Northern Ireland child sexual abuse cases represent approximately 20% of the total number of cases on the child abuse registers maintained by the Health and Social Services Boards.

8.92   The Northern Ireland strategy for dealing with the problem is as described in the response to Article 19 on child abuse.

8.93   In Scotland sexual offences come under common law as well as statute law, notably the Sexual Offences (Scotland) Act 1980 and the Civic Government (Scotland) Act 1982.

Sale, trafficking and abduction - Article 35

8.94   Under the Sexual Offences Act 1956 it is an offence to procure a girl under the age of 21 to have unlawful sexual intercourse with a third person anywhere in the world or to procure a woman or girl to become in any part of the world, a common prostitute or to procure her to leave the UK or her usual place of abode in the UK intending her to become an inmate of or to frequent a brothel for the purposes of prostitution.   Anyone who takes a child from those who have lawful control of that child commits an offence under the Child Abduction Act 1984. Alternatively, the common law of kidnapping may be relevant. The UK government is not aware that there is any evidence that children are being sold or taken from the UK for sexual purposes.

8.95   Under international law, the UK Government is not entitled to afford protection to our nationals who have dual nationality when they are in the country of their second nationality.

8.96   Any domestic servant accompanying their employers to the UK from abroad must be aged seventeen or over in order to qualify for entry. They must have been in continuous service with the same employer for at least twelve months prior to entering the UK, and have a valid entry clearance for that purpose. This must be obtained from an overseas post prior to travel to the UK. For an under-aged domestic servant to enter the UK as a family member would entail the use of duplicity in order to circumvent the rules. The UK immigration authorities as well as visa/consular staff at British posts overseas scrupulously apply immigration laws to all applications for entry clearance for visits to or settlement in, the UK.

Children belonging to a minority or an indigenous group - Article 30

8.97 Every person in the UK has the right to enjoy his or her own culture, to profess and practise his or her own religion and to use his or her own language. However, with over 200 minority languages used in the UK it would be both impractical and too costly for the UK to provide, as of right, translations of public correspondence and proceeding in all minority languages. In Wales, the Welsh Language Act 1993 establishes the principle that in the conduct of public business and the administration of justice the Welsh language should be treated on a basis of equality with English. The Act confirms and builds on the Government's long-running and continuing policy of support for the Welsh language.

Northern Ireland

8.98 In December 1992 the Central Community Relations Unit published a consultative document on race relations in Northern Ireland which examined the scope for legislation and considered what other steps Government might take further to promote equality and equity for ethnic minorities. Among issues likely to emerge are some which may particularly concern children and young persons in ethnic minority communities, including traditional Irish travellers. These include abuse and harassment, social isolation, problems in respect of educational attainment, difficulty in accessing social services and lack of adequate child care facilities.

8.99 The Unit also has responsibility for policy development in respect of the Irish language, which is set in the context of recognising and respecting the cultural identities of all sections of the community.

ANNEX A UK's Reservations and Declarations to the Convention

Immigration and Nationality

I   The United Kingdom reserves the right to apply such legislation, in so far as it relates to the entry into, stay in and departure from the United Kingdom of those who do not have the right under the law of the United Kingdom to enter and remain in the United Kingdom, and to the acquisition and possession of citizenship, as it may deem necessary from time to time.

Young Offenders

II   Where at any time there is a lack of suitable accommodation or adequate facilities for a particular individual in any institution in which young offenders are detained, or where the mixing of adults and children is deemed to be mutually beneficial, the United Kingdom reserves the right not to apply Article 37(c) in so far as those provisions require children who are detained to be accommodated separately from adults.

Definition of "child"

III   The United Kingdom interprets the Convention as applicable only following a live birth.

Definition of "parent"

IV   The United Kingdom interprets the references in the Convention to "parents" to mean only those persons who, as a matter of national law, are treated as parents. This includes cases where the law regards a child as having only one parent, for example where a child has been adopted by one person only and in certain cases where a child is conceived other than as a result of sexual intercourse by the woman who gives birth to it and she is treated as the only parent.

Young workers

V   Employment legislation in the United Kingdom does not treat persons under 18, but over the school-leaving age as children, but as "young people". Accordingly the United Kingdom reserves the right to continue to apply Article 32 subject to such employment legislation.

Children's hearings

VI   In Scotland there are tribunals (known as "children's hearings") which consider the welfare of the child and deal with the majority of offences which a child is alleged to have committed. In some cases, mainly of a welfare nature, the child is temporarily deprived of its liberty for up to seven days prior to attending the hearing. The child and its family are, however, allowed access to a lawyer during this period. Although the decisions of the hearings are subject to appeal to the courts, legal representation is not permitted at the proceedings of the children's hearings themselves. Children's hearings have proved over the years to be a very effective way of dealing with the problems of children in a less formal, non-adversarial manner. Accordingly, the United Kingdom, in respect of Article 37(d), reserves its right to continue the present operation of children's hearings.

Printed in the United Kingdom for HMSO
Dd 297645 C3.8 3/94 65536 08/29326